Nlp

How to Structure Success and Create Influence

(Life Changing Techniques for Personal and Professional Success)

Lyle Mitchell

Published By **Phil Dawson**

Lyle Mitchell

All Rights Reserved

Nlp: How to Structure Success and Create Influence (Life Changing Techniques for Personal and Professional Success)

ISBN 978-1-7777614-6-2

No part of this guidebook shall be reproduced in any form without permission in writing from the publisher except in the case of brief quotations embodied in critical articles or reviews.

Legal & Disclaimer

The information contained in this book is not designed to replace or take the place of any form of medicine or professional medical advice. The information in this book has been provided for educational & entertainment purposes only.

The information contained in this book has been compiled from sources deemed reliable, and it is accurate to the best of the Author's knowledge; however, the Author cannot guarantee its accuracy and validity and cannot be held liable for any errors or omissions. Changes are periodically made to this book. You must consult your doctor or get professional medical advice before using any of the suggested remedies, techniques, or information in this book.

Upon using the information contained in this book, you agree to hold harmless the Author from and against any damages, costs, and expenses, including any legal fees potentially resulting from the application of any of the information provided by this guide. This disclaimer applies to any damages or injury caused by the use and application, whether directly or indirectly, of any advice or information presented, whether for breach of contract, tort, negligence, personal injury, criminal intent, or under any other cause of action.

You agree to accept all risks of using the information presented inside this book. You need to consult a professional medical practitioner in order to ensure you are both able and healthy enough to participate in this program.

Table Of Contents

Chapter 1: Fundamentals Of Neuro Linguistic Programming 1

Chapter 2: Identification Of Negative Patterns 7

Chapter 3: Observation And Self-Awareness Techniques 15

Chapter 4: Changing Patterns With Nlp . 27

Chapter 5: Neuro Linguistic Programming And Visualization 35

Chapter 6: Effective Communication With Nlp 47

Chapter 7: Integration And Maintenance Of Change 75

Chapter 8: Practical Examples 87

Chapter 9: Nlp For Personal Development 109

Chapter 10: Nlp For Business And Leadership 125

Chapter 11: Nlp For Sports Performance Enhancement.. 139

Chapter 12: Nlp For Overcoming Phobias And Fears.. 156

Chapter 13: Nlp For Relationship And Communication Skills............................ 167

Chapter 14: Nlp For Stress Management And Anxiety Reduction.......................... 178

Chapter 1: Fundamentals Of Neuro Linguistic Programming

1. Explanation of the Basic Concepts of NLP

Undoubtedly, the conceptual framework of Neuro Linguistic Programming (NLP) is captivating and promising. In this primary bankruptcy, we find out its foundations, statistics how the ones requirements can be carried out to catalyze first rate trade in our lives.

NLP lets in us to decipher the codes of our thoughts, therefore supplying an operational guide to recognize how we technique the arena round us and the manner, in flip, our perceptions and mind form our movements and results. At the coronary heart of NLP lies the idea that we're the architects of our very own fact; that with the beneficial resource of reconfiguring our sorts of concept and behavior, we are able to redirect the path of our lives closer to a horizon of achievement and well-being.

One of its fundamental standards is modeling. This idea indicates that we're capable of version the cognitive and behavioral techniques of successful people and, with the resource of integrating these strategies into our private repertoire, we can accelerate our path in the direction of private and expert success. NLP presents the crucial system and techniques to decipher and reflect these models of excellence, as a quit end result facilitating a tangible direction to the popular change.

Another fundamental pillar is robust communique. It teaches us that the great of our communication with ourselves and others has a right away impact at the high-quality of our results.

By improving our conversation competencies, we're capable of cultivate extra enriching relationships and accumulate our desires extra efficiently.

Furthermore, it emphasizes the significance of cognitive and behavioral flexibility. In a constantly converting worldwide, the potential to conform and reply creatively to rising demanding situations is valuable. NLP gives a fixed of techniques that promote flexibility and resilience, allowing individuals to navigate lifestyles with extra self belief and competence.

NLP isn't always truly an precis idea but a living, applicable location that gives a strong set of equipment and techniques for self-discovery and personal transformation. Through the conscious exploration and application of its standards, humans can unlock latent capacity and forge a direction inside the direction of a greater enjoyable and sizeable life.

2. How Thoughts and Mental Patterns Influence Our Life

Undoubtedly, the relationship between our mind and highbrow patterns with the truth we enjoy is a essential element within the take a look at of Neuro Linguistic Programming (NLP). This interplay now not incredible shapes our belief of the arena but also dictates the first rate and path of our lives.

The impact of mind and mental patterns on our existence is profound and multifaceted. These cognitive systems act as filters thru which we interpret truth, and therefore, determine our responses and actions in the face of situations we come upon. A recurring bad idea, for instance, can restriction our capacity to look possibilities and make accurate choices. On the alternative hand, a great and high quality intellectual pattern can increase our horizon, allowing for additonal assertive motion and focus towards our desires.

Identifying our intellectual styles is the primary vital step closer to self-reflected picture and high excellent exchange. By being privy to how our mind have an impact on our actions, we are able to begin to form a truth that aligns with our goals and aspirations.

In precis, the recognition and conscious trade of our intellectual patterns, facilitated via NLP techniques, are critical techniques that permit human beings to exert greater control over their lives, transferring proactively in the direction of the belief of their aspirations. In this financial disaster, we've were given were given underscored the essential significance of knowledge and shaping our highbrow shape to correctly navigate the route to fulfillment and nicely-being.

3. The Importance of Internal and External Communication

Communication is a cornerstone inside the framework of Neuro Linguistic Programming (NLP). We delve into the spectrum of each inner and outdoor communique, exploring how the ones dimensions have interaction and form our non-public and professional reality.

1. Internal Communication

Internal Dialogue: Internal communication refers back to the communique we've got with ourselves. A healthy and constructive internal talk is critical for maintaining a top notch outlook and strong self-efficacy. NLP offers tools to domesticate an enriching internal speak, that would result in extra mental clarity, self notion, and effectiveness in preference-making.

Clarity of Objectives: Clarity in our inner communication is likewise pondered in the clean definition of our dreams and aspirations. By preserving effective internal verbal exchange, we will better align our moves with our dreams.

Chapter 2: Identification Of Negative Patterns

In this bankruptcy, we can delve into the critical undertaking of identifying terrible belief styles that may restrict our growth and well-being. I will offer you with the critical system to understand and recognize those patterns, your first step in the direction of alternate and private improvement.

2.1. How to Recognize Negative Thought Patterns

Identifying negative belief patterns is the number one crucial step for private exchange and growth. These styles are like highbrow conduct that would keep us trapped in cycles of restricting wondering and terrible emotions. Here we show you how to understand them:

2.1.1 Self-attention: Self-reputation is high to recognizing terrible styles. Start via listening to your mind and emotions especially conditions. Ask yourself the way you experience and what you are thinking at some stage in moments of pressure, anxiety, or dissatisfaction.

2.1.2 Key Words and Phrases: Observe the terms and phrases you typically use to your inner talk. Expressions which embody "continually", "in no way", "can not", or "want to" often advocate terrible styles. For instance, if you say "I am by no means accurate sufficient", you are revealing a horrible idea pattern related to vanity.

2.1.3 Repetitive Emotions: Identify the emotions that you enjoy regularly. Emotions such as normal worry, fear, or self-complaint can suggest bad idea patterns. If you experience irritating or depressed constantly, there may be an underlying pattern that desires to be addressed.

2.1.Four Triggering Situations: Reflect at the precise conditions that motive lousy mind. For example, do you revel in insecure in social situations? Are you continuously concerned about the future? Identifying triggering conditions will assist you apprehend styles in motion.

2.1.5 Self-Criticism Patterns: Excessive self-grievance is a common pattern. If you are too tough on yourself and continuously blame your self for errors or failures, you're experiencing a awful pattern that could limit your growth.

Practical Example: Recognizing a Negative Thought Pattern

Imagine that you are searching out a latest technique and have sent severa pastime applications without getting any responses. You begin having recurrent mind like: "They will in no manner hire me, I am a failure". In this situation:

The key phrase is "they'll never lease me".

The recurrent emotion is hopelessness.

The triggering scenario is the shortage of responses in your manner applications.

By spotting this sample, you may start to query its validity and search for techniques to trade it.

In the upcoming chapters, you may learn how to use strategies to replace the ones horrific patterns with greater excellent and tremendous thoughts and beliefs, if you need to let you redesign your life and collect your desires.

2.2 Examples of Common Limiting Thoughts

Limiting mind are beliefs that restrict us, save you us from moving in advance, and can undermine our self-self notion.

Often, those thoughts are irrational or unfounded, but they could have a strong effect on our feelings and moves. Here are some examples of common proscribing thoughts:

2.2.1 I am no longer well enough: This restricting idea could have an effect to your arrogance and self assure in your self. You also can experience which you are not as a good deal as par at paintings, to your relationships, or in any region of your lifestyles.

2.2.2 I can't do it: This perception makes you doubt your functionality to stand demanding situations. It can lead you to keep away from boom possibilities or to procrastinate in phrases of vital responsibilities.

2.2.Three Success is for others: This concept leads you to simply accept as real with that success is unbelievable for you and is exceptional intended for top notch people. You can also brush aside your private achievements and opportunities.

2.2.Four I continually fail: When you're taking delivery of as actual with that failure is regular in your lifestyles, you can expand a defeatist mentality that forestalls you from persevering to your desires.

2.2.5 I don't deserve love/happiness/achievement: This restricting idea could have an effect on your private relationships and your selected delight in lifestyles. It makes you enjoy that you do not deserve the notable matters that existence has to offer.

2.2.6 I want to be top notch: The relentless pursuit of perfection can be paralyzing. This restricting perception can generate tension and frustration even as you fail to meet your very own unrealistically immoderate expectancies.

2.2.7 I cannot change: Believing that you can not change or enhance may be one of the most adverse limiting mind. It prevents you from growing and studying out of your evaluations.

2.2.8 The global is in opposition to me: This concept leads you to sense like a victim of instances, which can create a experience of helplessness and resentment.

Practical Example: Overcoming a Limiting Thought

Imagine you've got the proscribing concept 'I am now not properly sufficient to be promoted at artwork'. This concept can result in lack of self assurance and a loss of initiative on your profession. To triumph over it, you may:

Identify evidence that challenges this idea, consisting of preceding achievements for your job.

Replace it with a greater excessive fine notion, which incorporates "I sincerely have precious capabilities that I can make a contribution to my employer".

Take concrete actions to illustrate your nicely well well worth and are attempting to find out expert improvement opportunities.

By recognizing and addressing those proscribing mind, you can unfastened yourself from self-imposed rules and skip toward your goals with self warranty.

In the following chapters, we're able to explore strategies that may be used to trade those horrific concept patterns and foster exquisite personal growth.

Chapter 3: Observation And Self-Awareness Techniques

In this bankruptcy, we are able to immerse ourselves within the captivating worldwide of announcement and self-cognizance. You will research effective strategies to boom your self-focus and better apprehend your concept and conduct styles, so that you can let you take control of your existence more successfully.

As you development, you will be empowered to perceive and understand your notion and conduct styles, offering you with a sturdy foundation for non-public change and non-forestall development. Get ready for an thrilling exploration of your own internal international!

three.1. Tools to Increase Self-Awareness

Self-consciousness(1) is an essential thing for figuring out and changing terrible belief patterns and restricting behaviors. The extra aware we're of our thoughts, emotions, and reactions, the more efficaciously we're able to interfere and make top notch modifications in our lives. Here we present a few equipment and strategies to growth self-popularity:

3.1.2 Keep a Journal of Thoughts and Emotions

Keeping a mag is one of the only gadget for growing self-attention. Record your mind, emotions, and triggering situations at some stage in the day.

By reviewing your magazine, you may be able to end up aware of horrible concept patterns and recurrent feelings. This will will allow you to take steps to trade them

(1) Self-interest refers to the functionality to understand oneself, being privy to oneself. It may be progressed via meditation, yoga, and other practices that sell mindfulness, along with mindfulness itself.

three.1.Three Meditation and Mindfulness

Meditation and mindfulness allow you to awareness on the winning and feature a examine your thoughts and emotions without judgment. These practices allow you to take distance from your automatic patterns.

Daily meditation will can help you increase greater self-recognition and decrease automated reactivity to horrific emotions.

three.1.Four Ask "Why?", "What for?"

Question your mind and emotions. When confronted with a terrible concept, ask your self 'Why am I wondering this?' or 'What made me feel this manner?, What am I reading for?.

By delving into the start of your thoughts and emotions, you will be capable of discover underlying ideals and past reports that may be fueling them.

three.1.Five Practice Self-Reflection

Dedicate time often to mirror on your existence, your goals, and your values. Ask yourself if your moves and mind are regular with what you absolutely need.

Self-reflected picture helps you to make more aware decisions and to become aware about areas for development.

three.1.6 Seek External Feedback

Sometimes, it is tough to be honestly aware about our private tendencies. Ask close to friends or mentors to offer you sincere comments on your concept and conduct patterns.

External comments can offer an purpose thoughts-set that we often forget about.

three.1.7 Self-Assessment Techniques

Use questionnaires or self-cognizance tests, which includes the Enneagram take a look at or the personal values questionnaire. These system can offer valuable insights into your character and center values.

Understanding your very personal technique and values will assist you are making decisions which is probably greater aligned collectively together with your real self.

3.2 Practical Exercises to Identify Negative Patterns

Practical sports activities are powerful equipment for growing self-attention and recognizing terrible thought styles. Here is a list of ten sporting activities that you may perform to grow to be privy to those styles in your life:

3.2.1 The Limiting Thoughts Journal

For one week, maintain a completely unique mag in which you document all mind you recognize as terrible or restricting. Note the date and the situation in which they passed off.

3.2.2 Emotion Map

Create an emotion map in that you word down the manner you sense at particular instances of the day. Then, find out concept patterns that coincide with certain feelings.

3.2.3 Three through Three

Select 3 important regions of your lifestyles, which include paintings, private relationships, and health. For one week, file three terrible mind associated with each of these areas.

3.2.Four The Detective Game

Every time you seize yourself wondering some factor horrible, act like a detective and search for proof that enables or refutes that concept. Is it truly actual? Are there any proofs to lower back it up?

three.2.Five Interview Yourself

Ask yourself introspective questions which embody 'Why am I questioning this way?' and 'Where does this idea come from?'. Write down your solutions to delve deeper into the starting area of your horrible styles.

three.2.6 The Trigger Situations Log

Keep an intensive document of conditions that cause horrible thoughts. Note the time, region, people worried, and what emerge as happening.

three.2.7 Key Words and Phrases

Identify key phrases and terms which you use on your bad mind. Write down those phrases and look for more effective alternatives.

three.2.Eight Beliefs Comparison

Make a listing of your modern-day ideals and evaluation them with more super ideals which you would like to adopt. This will assist you visualize the change you choice.

3.2.Nine Restructuring Questions

Every time you recognize a terrible concept, ask yourself restructuring questions, together with 'Is this beneficial?' or 'How can I view this from a more superb perspective?'

three.2.10 External Feedback

Ask close to buddies or own family to provide you with honest feedback on bad idea styles they've located in you.

3.2.Eleven Weekly Evaluation

At the surrender of each week, look at your logs and look for ordinary styles. Are there particular problems or conditions that frequently trigger terrible patterns?

These practical bodily video video games will help you understand terrible idea styles and increase yourself-recognition. As you advantage greater clarity on these patterns, you will be better organized to address them and update them with extra wonderful thoughts and ideals the usage of the strategies that we will find out within the following chapters.

3.Three. The Importance of Keeping a Thought Record

Keeping a idea file is a powerful tool for increasing self-recognition and recognizing bad belief patterns. A primarily based file permits you to check and have a study your thoughts in more element. Here I provide you with a guide on a manner to hold a notion record and an Excel desk that you may use for this reason.

Steps to Keep a Thought Record

1. Choose a pocket e-book or use an Excel spreadsheet to create your idea record.

2. Set up a column for the date and time even as the concept took place. This will allow you to find out idea styles at specific times of the day.

three. Create a column for the situation or context. Note in that you had been, who you were with, and what come to be taking vicinity on the identical time as the idea happened.

4. Record the horrible concept. Write down the precise concept you had, ensuring to be smooth and precise.

five. Identify related feelings. Note the way you felt at that 2d. You can use terms like anxiety, unhappiness, anger, and many others.

6. Look for evidence that helps or refutes the belief. In a separate column, be conscious any

objective evidence you need to beneficial resource or refute the terrible perception. This will help you question its validity.

7. Ask restructuring questions. In a few unique column, formulate restructuring inquiries to venture the terrible idea. You can ask yourself if the idea is beneficial, if it's far realistic, or how you may view the state of affairs from a extra high excellent perspective.

8. Record a reassessment. Note if your mind-set has changed after using the restructuring questions. Have you come back to a one in all a type or greater balanced end?

9. Track styles. Regularly evaluation your concept report (e.G., weekly) to search for recurring patterns in situations, emotions, or terrible thoughts.

Example of an Excel desk for concept recording:

You can create an Excel table with the subsequent columns to hold an prepared report of mind:

nine " I am now not proper enough Previous Achievements in Presentations beneficial? What are my abilities I experience that I can deal with it with well enough preparation table will will permit you to systematically record and study your terrible thoughts, facilitating the identification of patterns and the software of restructuring techniques. Remember to study your document frequently to advantage a clearer insight into your idea and emotion styles [Restructuring Questions] keeping a journal in which you observe down your thoughts and feelings at a few degree in the day. Record specific events, triggering situations, and the way you felt in response to them.

After 15 days, evaluate your mag and look for styles. For example, you could locate that you commonly generally tend to feel traumatic in teamwork conditions. This gives you with treasured records approximately a probable proscribing perception pattern that you can address.

Increasing self-attention will can help you perceive and question your horrific concept patterns and, in the long run, provide you with the energy to alternate them.

In this financial disaster, we've got got delved into the paintings of remark and self-attention, mastering crucial tools and strategies to better understand our idea and conduct patterns. We spotlight three key factors:

Self-reputation is a effective device for non-public change and non-forestall development.

Observation strategies permit us to recognize our idea and conduct patterns.

Chapter 4: Changing Patterns With Nlp

In this monetary catastrophe, we will delve into the exciting assignment of changing perception and conduct patterns. You will research effective strategies and strategies so one can assist you to remodel additives of your existence that you want to enhance.

These strategies are based absolutely on the idea that we're able to reprogram our minds to accumulate more excessive great consequences.

We will discover in element the idea of anchors and the way they'll be used to exchange terrible emotional states to extra first-rate and useful ones.

We will look into the technique of reframing and the manner it can assist us alternate our views and perceptions of situations, considering greater adaptability and trouble-fixing.

You will accumulate valuable abilties for non-public transformation. As you delve deeper into those techniques, you will be higher organized to tackle and alternate concept and conduct patterns that formerly appeared hard to triumph over. Get ready to find out a international of opportunities and personal growth!

4.1. NLP Change Techniques

four.1.2 The Change Mindset

NLP starts offevolved with the critical belief that the mind is malleable and that we are able to trade our perception and behavior patterns if we are willing to acquire this. This consists of adopting a thoughts-set of openness and flexibility in the direction of change.

four.1.Three Continuous Observation and Awareness

Before you may exchange horrific patterns, it's miles essential to look at them and be aware of them. Self-attention is step one in the direction of exchange.

four.1.Three Effective Communication

Communication is important to exchange. This includes every communication with ourselves (our inner voice) and communication with others. Through NLP strategies, we learn how to speak more efficaciously to influence our mind and behaviors.

4.1.Four Replacing Negative Patterns

Once we've have been given recognized horrible concept patterns, NLP gives us with gadget to update them with extra quality and optimistic patterns. This includes difficult and questioning proscribing ideals and converting them with ideals that propel us towards our desires.

4.1.5 Anchoring Techniques

Anchoring techniques are used to associate precise emotional states with stimuli or actions. For example, you could create an 'anchor' that allows you enjoy assured earlier than an critical presentation.

4.1.6 Modeling Success

Another essential approach is modeling. This entails analyzing and studying from a achievement humans in unique areas to adopt their idea and behavior patterns. You can version the achievement of someone to your enterprise or situation of interest.

4.1.7 Creative Visualization

Creative visualization is used to application the thoughts for fulfillment. Through visualization, you may workout conditions to your mind earlier than going through them in real life, growing your self guarantee and competencies.

4.1.Eight Integration of Change

Changing styles isn't always pretty a great deal making short changes, however about integrating the ones modifications into your each day lifestyles. This consists of non-forestall exercising and consolidation of new strategies of questioning and performing.

In the following elements, we are able to discover in detail the ones change techniques and a way to apply them particularly situations.

4.2. Anchors and Their Application for Changing Emotional States

Anchors are a powerful approach used to companion precise emotional states with stimuli or actions. These emotional states can encompass self guarantee, calmness, motivation, and every one-of-a-kind desired u . S . A .. Here we deliver an cause of how anchors artwork and the manner you could practice them to trade your emotional states.

4.2.1. What is an Anchor?

An anchor is a connection or association amongst an outdoor stimulus and an inner emotional us of a. In incredible words, when you enjoy a specific emotional u . S . A . (for example, self belief), you may 'anchor' it to a particular stimulus, on the side of a gesture, a word, or an photo.

four.2.2. Creating Anchors

To create an anchor, look at the ones steps:

1. Choose a preferred emotional kingdom: Decide what emotional u.S. You want to anchor. It can be self notion, relaxation, enthusiasm, and so on.

2. Find the right 2d: Wait to revel in that emotional state clearly or recollect a time at the same time as you felt it intensely.

three. Create an anchoring stimulus: During the peak of that emotional kingdom, follow a particular stimulus, together with urgent your thumb and index finger together, announcing a key word or looking at an photograph.

4. Repeat the machine: Repeat this system severa times to boost the association a few of the emotional state and the anchoring stimulus.

4.2.Three. Application of anchors for the trade of emotional states.

Once you have were given created an anchor, you could use it to trade emotional states in specific situations. Here is an example of the way to exercise an anchor to growth self belief earlier than a presentation.

1. Prepare your anchor: Before the presentation, put together to apply your anchor. This might also involve urgent your thumb and index finger together.

2. Recall the preferred state: Recall a time whilst you felt pretty consistent and assured.

3. Apply the anchor: Just earlier than beginning the presentation, study your anchor (press your thumb and forefinger together). This will prompt the favored emotional united states of america of america of self guarantee.

4. Deliver the presentation: Deliver your presentation at the same time as maintaining the anchor. As you move alongside, the self warranty you have formerly anchored will

assist you face the situation extra with a chunk of good fortune.

five. Reinforce the anchor: After the presentation, reapply the anchor whilst congratulating yourself on your a fulfillment overall performance. This reinforces the affiliation amongst self guarantee and the anchor stimulus.

Anchors can be used to change a large variety of emotional states in pretty a few conditions.

This technique lets in you to have greater control over your emotions and intellectual states, which in flip assist you to triumph over terrible idea styles and restricting behaviors.

In the subsequent sections of this financial disaster, we can discover special techniques that complement anchoring for effective alternate.

Here are 10 realistic physical sports activities for growing and making use of anchors in high-quality situations:

Chapter 5: Neuro Linguistic Programming And Visualization

We will explore how Neuro Linguistic Programming (NLP) integrates with visualization and imagination to effect large changes in concept and behavior styles. Visualization and creativeness are powerful gadget that allow us to create clean and tremendous intellectual photos of our desires and objectives. Through those techniques, we are able to effect our beliefs, feelings, and actions to benefit great trade in our lives.

We will look at the "Perfect Future" approach, in case you need to let you do not forget a destiny in that you have already finished your desires. You will discover how this method can impact your unconscious thoughts and encourage you inside the route of success.

You will use effective present-demanding affirmations to boost your dreams and goals. You will create affirmations that decorate yourself guarantee and vanity.

I will offer you with the essential gear to apply visualization and creativeness correctly on your each day lifestyles. As you improvement within the ones necessities and strategies, you'll be higher organized to persuade your highbrow and emotional styles, and to benefit greater self-attention and private increase. Get equipped to unleash your capability and visualize a shiny destiny!

five.1. Use of visualization and creativeness to alternate patterns

Visualization and creativeness are important additives of NLP that allow us to:

Create a smooth popularity: Visualization permits us outline our desires and dreams simply, which in flip allows us to live targeted on them.

Generate terrific feelings: By imagining a success eventualities, we are able to experience great feelings along with self belief, motivation, and gratitude, which enhances our motivation and vanity.

Reprogram idea styles: Visualization permits us to replace terrible notion styles with notable and optimistic intellectual pictures.

Increase self-self notion: Visualizing situations wherein we are a fulfillment allows us expand extra self warranty in our abilties and capacities.

Overcome intellectual limitations: By visualizing overcoming traumatic situations, we are able to put together our mind to cope with difficult situations with a effective mind-set and determination.

Examples of Using Visualization and Imagination:

1. Visualization of Personal Goals: If you want to shed pounds, you can use visualization to expect yourself reaching your perfect weight. Create a smooth intellectual photograph of approaches you appearance and how you revel in at that weight, which can motivate you to make healthier selections.

2. Visualization of Professional Success: If you have got were given an critical mission at paintings, you may use visualization to anticipate every step of the system and visualize the very last fulfillment. This will assist you live focused and assured as you parent on the project.

three. Public Speaking Visualization: If you have a worry of public speakme, you may use visualization to assume your self within the the front of an target market, speaking with a chunk of luck and actually. This workout will assist you lessen tension earlier than a presentation.

4. Personal Relationships Visualization: If you desire to enhance your private relationships, you could use visualization to imagine effective and loving interactions with the human beings round you. This can help you change negative communication patterns.

5. Sports Success Visualization: If you practice a interest, you may use visualization to expect your well-known basic overall performance in

competitive situations. Visualize your movements and moves because it should be to decorate your actual general overall performance.

6. Relaxation Visualization: If you need to reduce strain, you could use visualization to create intellectual images of tranquil and enjoyable places, which consist of a seaside or a wooded location. Imagine every element and sensation to prompt relaxation.

Visualization and imagination are flexible gadget that can be finished in quite a few conditions to change concept and conduct patterns. As we development in this monetary catastrophe, we are able to find out precise visualization strategies and sensible sports sports that will help you make the most of these device on your everyday life.

Here I gift you with 10 sensible sporting activities of visualization and imagination strategies in Neuro Linguistic Programming (NLP)

Exercise 1: Professional Success Visualization

1. Close your eyes and visualize a scene in which you are reaching huge professional fulfillment.

2. Detail the factors of the scene, together along with your art work environment, the humans round you, and your successful movements.

three. Feel the satisfaction and satisfaction you revel in in that moment.

Exercise 2: Visualization of Rest and Relaxation

1. Imagine a non violent and exciting vicinity, which consist of a seashore or a woodland.

2. Visualize all of the information of that vicinity, which include the sounds, colorings, and bodily sensations.

3. Feel how relaxation spreads for the duration of your body as you immerse your self on this intellectual scene.

Exercise 3: Visualization of Success in Sports or Hobbies

1. If you exercise a exercise or a hobby, visualize an exceptional overall performance in your desired hobby.

2. See each motion and motion with precision, feeling the fluidity and mastery in what you do.

three. Feel the excitement and delight of having an extraordinary overall overall performance.

Exercise four: Visualization of Effective Communication

1. Imagine a verbal exchange in which you communicate actually and efficaciously.

2. Visualize how the alternative individual is aware and responds surely on your message.

three. Feel the self perception and satisfaction of a achievement conversation.

Exercise 5: Visualization of Personal Goals

1. Visualize a scene wherein you have got got finished actually virtually one of your non-public dreams.

2. Detail the way you revel in having completed that reason and the way it indicates in your existence.

3. Feel the gratitude and fulfillment in that 2nd.

Exercise 6: Visualization of Overcoming Challenges

1. Think about a current mission you are handling.

2. Visualize a scene in which you successfully and determinedly overcome that mission.

three. Feel the pride of having overcome the obstacle and self guarantee to your talents.

Exercise 7: Visualization of Positive Personal Relationships

1. Visualize an interplay with an critical character in your lifestyles in which the relationship is harmonious and loving.

2. Detail the manner you speak and experience in that interaction.

three. Feel the emotional connection and delight of having high superb relationships.

Exercise 8: Visualization of Success in Presentations

1. If you need to make a presentation, visualize the immediate you are within the the front of the target audience.

2. See the manner you communicate with self guarantee and clarity, taking pictures absolutely everyone's attention.

three. Feel the pleasure of getting delivered a successful presentation.

Exercise nine: Visualization of Travel and Adventures

1. Imagine an thrilling adventure or adventure you preference to adopt inside the destiny.

2. Visualize all of the records, from the holiday spot to the opinions you can have.

3. Feel the delight and anticipation of that future journey.

Exercise 10: Visualization of Creativity and Expression

1. If you are revolutionary, visualize a piece consultation wherein your creativity flows extensively.

2. See the way you generate innovative mind and the way they materialize to your work.

3. Feel the satisfaction and success of your creative expression.

These visualization and imagination bodily video games let you popularity on your dreams, trade concept styles, and make more potent your perception to your capability to advantage success in various regions of your lifestyles. Practice frequently for the first rate results.

5.2. "Perfect Future" Techniques in NLP

five.2.1. What is the "Perfect Future" in NLP?

"Perfect destiny" strategies in Neuro Linguistic Programming (NLP) are a effective method to using visualization and creativeness correctly. These strategies recognition on creating a shiny highbrow image of a future in which you have already completed your goals or objectives, permitting you to experience that success in an anticipatory and stimulating way. Next, we are capable of discover the way to observe those techniques and the way they are able to exchange concept and behavior styles:

five.2.2. Steps to Use the "Perfect Future"

Define your desires: Start via manner of way of certainly figuring out the dreams or goals you need to acquire. They may be personal, professional, or from any place of your lifestyles.

Visualize the fulfillment: Close your eyes and create an intensive intellectual photograph of your self within the destiny, having effectively finished your dreams. Imagine the information, together with in which you are, the way you revel in, and what subjects appear like at that second.

Involve your senses: Not only visualize but moreover have interaction your unique senses. What do you pay interest at that moment? What physical sensations do you revel in? How do you enjoy emotionally?

Feel the emotion: Experience the immoderate fine emotions associated with accomplishing your desires in that pleasant future. Feel the pride, satisfaction, and gratitude as if you had already reached your goals.

Chapter 6: Effective Communication With Nlp

In this financial disaster, we're capable of find out the significance of powerful verbal exchange and the way NLP can enhance our interpersonal verbal exchange talents. You will increase vital competencies to speak greater correctly together with your own family, colleagues, and buddies. As you take a look at those ideas and techniques to your existence, you will be capable of create deeper connections, take a look at from others in a meaningful way, and growth your relationships on a non-public and expert degree. Get prepared to improve your verbal exchange abilities and connect with others greater successfully!

6.1. How to Apply NLP to Improve Interpersonal Communication

Neuro Linguistic Programming (NLP) offers a treasured approach to enhancing interpersonal communique. In this primary phase, we are able to discover how you could take a look at NLP to strengthen your verbal exchange skills and create more effective connections with others.

6.1.2 Fundamental Principles of Effective Communication with NLP

6.1.2.1 Rapport

Rapport is the inspiration of all powerful communication. It refers to developing a robust and harmonious reference to the other person, which enables open and empathetic communique. To correctly set up rapport, it's far crucial to music in with the alternative person and create an surroundings of accept as true with.

This can be completed with the useful aid of:

Empathizing with their feelings: Actively pay interest and display know-how towards the possibility person's feelings and reviews.

Synchronizing body language, additionally referred to as mimicry: This refers back to the act of unconsciously imitating the gestures, facial expressions, postures, language patterns, and different behaviors of the person we're interacting with. This phenomenon is based totally on the basis that imitating someone can create a experience of empathy and connection a number of the people concerned in the communique.

Here are some approaches wherein mimicry can appear in verbal exchange:

Body Posture: Adopting a posture similar to our interlocutor's. If they lean forward, one can also lean barely beforehand.

Gestures: If the character we are speakme to uses pleasant hand gestures, we'd start to use similar gestures inside the communique.

Facial Expressions: Reflecting facial expressions like smiles, frowning, or displaying marvel.

Voice Tones: Adjusting the tone and quantity of our voice to healthful the alternative man or woman's.

Speech Patterns: Imitating the rhythm or tempo of the alternative character's speech.

Mimicry may be a effective device for boosting communique and reference to others. By mirroring the opportunity man or woman, we supply a subconscious message that we are in tune and in harmony with them. This can make the individual experience more understood and traditional, predominant to extra open and effective communique.

It is crucial to have a look at that mimicry must be diffused and natural; if exaggerated, it is able to be perceived as mocking or insincere, having the alternative effect within the interaction. Therefore, it have to be practiced with sensitivity and with the cause of constructing real rapport, no longer as a manipulation approach.

Example: Imagine you are talking to a patron who is concerned approximately a trouble with their product. You can create rapport through pronouncing: "I absolutely understand why you enjoy annoyed thru manner of this case. We are proper here to help you solve it".

We must summarize that Rapport is: the technique of constructing a relationship of agree with and mutual knowledge with every different individual. It is a harmonious connection in which human beings feel understood and frequent, facilitating more fluid verbal exchange. It is considered an crucial expertise for putting in top communique and is finished thru empathy and the mirrored photo or imitation of body posture, gestures, tone of voice, speech rhythm, among one in all a kind elements of non-verbal communication.

6.1.2.2 Calibración

Calibration involves taking note of the verbal and non-verbal cues of the opposite person to better apprehend their emotional country and verbal exchange. This permits you to adjust your technique and tailor your communique greater efficaciously. To obtain this, observe:

Detailed assertion: Pay interest to facial expressions, voice tone, gestures, and different non-verbal signs that offer you with clues about the man or woman's emotional united states of america.

Adjusting your method: If you recognize that the alternative man or woman is disturbing, you could adjust your communique to be greater reassuring and information.

Example: During a conversation, you phrase that the person is frowning and speakme in a louder tone. This may additionally need to indicate frustration or anger. You can calibrate your verbal exchange to be more affected individual and are attempting to find answers collectively.

In short, calibration is the method of reading the alternative person, searching, and know-how the non-verbal responses of the interlocutor to adjust one's conversation efficaciously. Calibrating approach being able to phrase the slightest conversation signs inside the distinctive man or woman, which include modifications in breathing, pores and pores and skin complexion, eye moves, gestures, and one-of-a-type clues which can propose how they feel or react to what is being stated.

Are they complementary or can they be used separately?

Rapport and calibration are complementary. Calibration can be used to decorate rapport, because the greater you can examine and recognize someone's non-verbal signs, the less tough it is going to be to alter your private behavior to bolster the reference to them. For instance, if upon calibrating we be conscious that our interlocutor is uncomfortable with a nice problem count number range of verbal exchange, we're capable of change the trouble to hold rapport.

On the alternative hand, despite the fact that they may be complementary, additionally they can be used independently. One should calibrate with out continually looking for rapport, absolutely as a manner to higher recognize the possibility character in a given context, like a negotiator reading the counterpart's alerts. Likewise, one need to try to installation rapport with someone through verbal exchange and empathetic frame language with out making an in depth calibration of all their responses.

Therefore, let's imagine that, at the same time as rapport focuses on constructing and preserving a harmonious dating, calibration concentrates at the statement and super-tuning of communique. They are skills that, notwithstanding the truth that one of a kind, art work thoroughly together to enhance the pleasant of human interactions.

6.1.2. Three Language Metamodel

The metamodel is based totally totally on the basis that the language we use displays our inner instance of the arena, however this illustration is continually confined with the resource of the shape of language itself. When we talk, we pass over statistics, distort opinions, and generalize data. Although that may be a regular part of the abstraction technique that allows people to anticipate and speak efficiently, it can additionally purpose misunderstandings and boundaries in our thinking.

The language metamodel is a device that permits you to ask specific questions to make clean communique and achieve greater precise records. It helps choose out out and accurate generalizations, omissions, and distortions within the exceptional character's language.

How is the Metamodel used?

In NLP, the metamodel is used to make clean language via asking the interlocutor inside the kind of manner that allows them bear in mind their enjoy in a extra precise and specific way.

Precise questions: Use questions like "What exactly does that advocate?" or "Can you deliver me an example?" to attain extra specific and awesome facts.

Open and closed questions: When referring to "open questions," we are talking approximately a selected type of questions which may be used to inspire deeper and greater precise conversation. Unlike closed questions, which could normally be responded with a "nice" or "no," open questions invite the opposite man or woman to proportion greater data, feelings, opinions, and personal reflections.

Example: Instead of asking "Did you want the place you traveled to?" (that is a closed query), you may ask "What did you like maximum about the place you traveled to and why?" (this is an open question). Open questions often start with "what," "how," "while," "in which," or "who," and are a key device in lively listening due to the fact they display real interest in what the other character is announcing and inspire richer and more full-size communique.

Clarification of vague requirements: If someone says "It constantly happens to me," you could ask "Always? Can you preserve in thoughts a specific example?"

Example: During a piece communique, a colleague says: "I never get assist in this mission." You can observe the language metamodel through way of using asking: "Never? Is there a selected incident in that you did now not get keep of guide?"

6.1.2. Four Visual and Auditory Access Cues

People manner data via wonderful sensory channels: seen, auditory, and kinesthetic. By figuring out which channel is important in a person, you may tailor your verbal exchange to be more powerful.

Visual: Visual human beings regularly use terms and phrases associated with sight, which incorporates "I see what you imply" or "That seems easy".

Auditory: Auditory people attention on sound and might use expressions like "I heard what you stated" or "That sounds tremendous".

Example: During a assembly, you will probably phrase that a colleague uses terms like "I do now not see the hassle" and "Look at it from this perspective." This indicates a seen technique of their information processing, so that you can tailor your communication by using way of the usage of visible examples and metaphors related to sight to be greater powerful in conveying your message.

Kinesthetic: Kinesthetic human beings enjoy and undergo in mind the area round them through frame sensations and emotions. Often, these sorts of humans speak approximately their feelings and sensations, the usage of expressions like "I feel cushty with this" or "That touches me." Kinesthetic descriptions can also embody references to bodily movement, like "grabbing an opportunity" or "transferring inside the direction of a reason."

You can find out a kinesthetic individual via the terms and terms they use, which often reference physical sensations or emotional states. Additionally, those sorts of humans may also moreover price practical enjoy and getting to know through fingers-on workout and direct touch with materials or the surroundings.

6.1. Three Practical Exercises to Improve Communication

Practicing rapport is essential to enhancing our functionality to connect with others. Here are some sporting sports activities and sports that could help:

6.1.Three.1 Rapport Exercises

Exercise 1: Gesture Mirroring

Step 1: Find a partner to exercising this exercise.

Step 2: Sit head to head and choose roles of "A" and

"B".

Step 3: Participant "A" will mimic the gestures and moves of player "B" subtly and really.

Step four: Switch roles and permit "B" mimic "A".

Step five: After a few minutes, mirror on the way you felt in some unspecified time in the future of the interest and communicate how diffused imitation can create a feel of connection and attunement in some unspecified time in the future of communique. This is rapport.

Exercise 2: Shared Stories

Step 1: Find a accomplice and sit down resultseasily.

Step 2: Each of you shares a non-public anecdote or a massive story from your existence.

Step 3: As you listen to the opposite's tale, try to emotionally connect to their enjoy and show empathy.

Step four: After both recollections, reflect on the manner you felt sharing and the way empathy strengthened the connection.

Exercise 3: Active Listening to Stories

Step 1: Ask a pal or family member to share a personal enjoy or story with you.

Step 2: Listen attentively, asking open questions to delve into the data.

Step three: At the prevent of the conversation, summarize the story and show knowledge.

In the context of workout 3, step 2 encourages the listener to apply open-ended inquiries to better understand and accumulate extra records approximately the story being shared by way of the usage of using their friend or family member. This now not handiest lets in the person telling the tale to mirror and likely find out new insights approximately their very very own revel in, however it moreover indicates that the listener is honestly fascinated and engaged in records and validating the opportunity's emotions and views.

Exercise 4: Shared Key Words

Step 1: In a conversation, grow to be aware about the key phrases that the opposite person often makes use of.

Step 2: Use the ones identical key phrases in your response to illustrate attunement and connection.

Step three: Observe how the opportunity individual responds to the similarity in language.

Exercise 5: Simulation of Shared Interests

Step 1: Identify a subject of shared interest with someone.

Step 2: Practice a conversation in which both individuals show enthusiasm for the concern and collectively help each exceptional in exploring the hassle.

6.1.Three.2 Calibration Exercises

Exercise 1: Active Listening

Step 1: Choose a friend or member of the family to speak to.

Step 2: While speaking, exercising lively listening thru being attentive to facial expressions, voice tone, and other non-verbal signs and signs and symptoms.

Step three: Ask open-ended inquiries to accumulate more statistics and display your interest of their enjoy.

Step four: After the verbal exchange, mirror on what you found and the way calibration helped you better recognize their emotional america of the united states.

Exercise 2: Detecting Changes in State

Step 1: In a verbal exchange, be aware about subtle adjustments in the exceptional character's emotional country.

Step 2: Ask questions to find out how they sense at specific moments in the conversation.

Exercise 3: Emotions Over the Phone

Step 1: Have a cellular telephone conversation with a person and interest on detecting emotions through their tone of voice.

Step 2: Ask questions to validate your observations and better understand their emotional kingdom.

Exercise 4: The Microexpression Game

Step 1: Observe the facial microexpressions of human beings in a meeting or interaction.

Step 2: Try to pick out the emotions that those microexpressions mirror.

Exercise five: Calibration of Sensory Preferences

Step 1: Practice detecting humans's sensory alternatives based totally mostly on their desire of phrases (visible, auditory, kinesthetic)

Step 2: Adjust your language to reflect their desire and look at the way it influences verbal exchange.

Exercise 6: Calibration of Speech Rhythm

Step 1: In a verbal exchange, be aware about the other character's speech rhythm.

Step 2: Adjust your personal speech rhythm to synchronize with the alternative person's and have a look at the manner it affects the interplay.

Exercise 7: Calibration with a Partner

Objective: To enhance the functionality to take a look at and react to non-verbal cues in direct interplay.

Preparation: Work with a accomplice. Decide who can be the signal emitter and who may be the observer.

Signal Emission: The emitter want to undertake a series of emotions, one after the other (as an example, pride, unhappiness, surprise), and specific them pleasant with body language and facial expressions.

Observation and Feedback: The observer ought to describe what they see and deduce the emotion that the emitter is trying to talk.

After each attempt, the emitter offers remarks on the accuracy of the observer's reading.

6.1.Three.3 Language Metamodel Exercises

Exercises of the language metamodel can help deepen verbal exchange and task ambiguities, generalizations, and distortions in language.

Exercise 1: Clarifying Communication

Step 1: Think about a modern communication in which conversation modified into puzzling or ambiguous.

Step 2: Make a listing of unique questions based truely on the language metamodel that you may have used to make easy the communication.

Step three: Practice asking those questions with a friend or in a simulated scenario.

Step four: Reflect on how the questions helped to obtain clearer information.

Exercise 2: Deciphering Generalizations

Step 1: Listen to a communication or speech and look for generalizations or indistinct phrases used by the speaker.

Step 2: Formulate particular questions based totally on the language metamodel to make clean those generalizations and reap concrete information.

Exercise 3: Recognizing Omissions

Step 1: Read a piece of writing or be aware about a presentation where critical information or records are overlooked.

Step 2: Practice identifying the omissions and formulate inquiries to fill within the gaps.

Exercise 4: Exploring Distortions

Step 1: Have a communication wherein a person makes use of cognitive distortions, along with exaggerations or assumption.

Step 2: Use the language metamodel to invite questions that help the individual see the situation from a extra aim mind-set.

Exercise five: Creating Clarification Questions

Step 1: Listen to a verbal exchange in which conversation is not easy.

Step 2: Practice growing rationalization questions the use of the language metamodel to enhance know-how.

Exercise 6: Application of the Metamodel in Writing

Step 1: Write a tale or description that consists of generalizations, omissions, or distortions.

Step 2: Review your writing and feature a look at the language metamodel to enhance clarity and precision.

6.1.Three.4 Exercises on Visual and Auditory Access Cues

Exercise 1: Discovering the Predominant Channel

Step 1: Observe the people for your environment and be aware about the terms and phrases they use maximum regularly in their verbal exchange.

Step 2: Classify humans into three training: seen, auditory, and kinesthetic, primarily based absolutely on the access cues you perceive.

Step 3: Practice adapting your verbal exchange in line with the important channel of the person you are interacting with

Step four: Reflect on how model improved statistics and conversation in your interactions.

Exercise 2: Strengthening Visual and Auditory Communication

Step 1: Choose a conversation scenario, in conjunction with a presentation or an critical communication.

Step 2: Prepare your message using metaphors and seen examples in case you are speaking with a visual goal market, or use auditory examples if you are communicating with an auditory goal marketplace.

Step three: Deliver your message and have a look at the reactions and understanding of your audience.

Step four: Reflect on how the choice of seen or auditory method impacted the effectiveness of your communique.

Exercise 3: Reinforcing Visual Cues

Step 1: In a conversation, have a take a look at the visible cues the alternative person makes use of (as an instance, "I see what you recommend")

Step 2: Respond the use of visual expressions and metaphors associated with sight to reinforce the conversation.

Exercise 4: Visual Description

Step 1: Choose an object and describe it the usage of seen sensory language, focusing on shades, shapes, and facts.

Step 2: Ask another person to close their eyes and be privy to the define, searching for to visualise the object.

Step 3: Share your studies and observe how vibrant the highbrow photo grow to be.

Exercise five: Exploring the Auditory Channel

Step 1: Identify a person who has a bent to apply auditory cues of their language (as an example, "Sounds correct to me").

Step 2: Practice adapting your communique the use of auditory expressions and examples associated with sound

Exercise 6: Auditory Narration

Step 1: Share a private revel in the usage of auditory sensory language, describing sounds and rhythms.

Step 2: Ask the alternative individual to close their eyes and be aware of the narration, trying to experience the sounds.

Step three: Share your impressions on how auditory data enriched the enjoy.

Exercise 7: Multichannel Communication

Step 1: In a meeting or communication, be aware of the visual and auditory cues that human beings use of their communique.

Step 2: Adapt your reaction the use of expressions and examples that deal with every channels to bolster know-how.

Exercise 8: Creation of Visual Metaphors

Step 1: Choose a topic or idea and create a visual metaphor to offer an motive for it.

Step 2: Share the metaphor in a verbal exchange and test the way it improves the records of others.

Exercise nine: Auditory Narration of Experiences

Step 1: Share a personal enjoy the use of an intensive oral narration.

Step 2: Ask someone to pay attention to you after which percentage their impressions on the way it helped them hook up with your experience.

These sports activities will assist you support your abilities in rapport, calibration, language metamodel, and visual and auditory get right of entry to cues, permitting you to speak more correctly and higher recognize human beings in various conditions.

6.1. Four Techniques to Improve Communication

6.1.Four.1 Pacing and Leading

It is a essential approach in NLP that allows you to installation and maintain a robust reference to the other person after which direct the conversation in the direction of your desires without growing resistance. The steps and way are specific underneath:

Step 1: Pacing (Synchronizing)

Pacing consists of synchronizing with the other individual. Start via subtly and actually adopting elements in their conduct, collectively with body language, tone of voice, and speech rhythm.

Pay hobby to their key phrases and communique style. Reflect the ones key phrases and versions on your very private language.

Chapter 7: Integration And Maintenance Of Change

In this bankruptcy, we delve into the very last and crucial stage of our journey thru Neuro Linguistic Programming (NLP): the integration and protection of exchange. As you have got were given explored the numerous techniques and concepts in the course of this ebook, you have were given were given obtained a treasured set of device to decorate your communique, trade restricting belief patterns, and gain your dreams. Now, you can discover ways to make sure that those modifications become eternal in your lifestyles.

You will find out the way to:

Consolidate Changes: You will take a look at strategies to make certain that the adjustments you have got were given performed the use of NLP emerge as part of your new truth. Consolidation is top to heading off relapses and preserving development.

Integrate NLP into Your Daily Life: I will provide you with sensible recommendations on a manner to contain the strategies into your every day regular, so they emerge as natural and effective conduct.

Overcome Obstacles and Resistances: We will address capability obstacles and resistances you may face whilst imposing NLP on your life and offer you with strategies to conquer them.

Establish Long-Term Goals: You will learn how to define and paintings inside the course of long-time period goals which may be aligned collectively collectively along with your deepest values and goals.

Maintain Motivation and Self-Confidence: We will discover a way to maintain your motivation and self-self notion excessive as you improvement to your path of exchange and private boom.

7.1. How to Integrate New Thought and Behavior Patterns

Once you have were given were given located and finished numerous techniques to trade idea and behavior styles, it is critical to understand a way to correctly integrate those adjustments into your each day life. Integration guarantees that the cutting-edge styles emerge as natural and continual. Here's a manner to do it:

Step 1: Reflection and Acknowledgment

Before starting the mixing method, make an effort to reflect at the adjustments you've got finished. Recognize your accomplishments and function a laugh your development. This will beef up your willpower and motivation.

Step 2: Set Up Visual and Auditory Reminders

An effective way to combine new styles is to apply visual and auditory reminders. You can try this in the following techniques:

Affirm your dreams: Create written affirmations or document affirmations with your voice to concentrate to them every day.

These affirmations ought to reflect the adjustments you want to preserve.

Vision board: Create a vision board with photos and terms that represent your dreams and new styles. Place it in a seen area.

Step three: Practice Regularly

Constant workout is essential to integration. Dedicate time to training the strategies which have helped to procure the exchange. This will make stronger the brand new patterns and turn them into habits.

Step 4: Set Long-Term Goals

Define prolonged-time period goals that align with the changes you preference to keep. These desires will provide you with a revel in of path and a motive to maintain strolling on your personal improvement.

Step 5: Learn from Relapses

It's normal to enjoy relapses inside the exchange technique. Instead of having discouraged, use these critiques as analyzing possibilities. Reflect on what delivered about them and make bigger strategies to keep away from them inside the destiny.

Step 6: Seek Support

Share your integration dreams with pals, circle of relatives, or an NLP therapist. Support and duty may be critical for maintaining trade.

Step 7: Be Flexible

As you improvement, you could discover greater effective ways to enforce your new styles. Be flexible and inclined to adjust your approach as wanted.

Successful integration of latest concept and behavior patterns requires time and non-prevent attempt. By following the ones steps and preserving a constant awareness in your desires, you'll be on the right path to make sure that the changes come to be a eternal and useful part of your life. You have already got the device; now it is as plenty as you to use them effectively.

7.1.2 Practical Exercises for Integrating New Thought and Behavior Patterns

1. Daily Success Log:

Step 1: Keep a magazine in which you document each day successes experienced whilst making use of your new concept and conduct styles.

Step 2: Reflect at the way you felt and which techniques worked quality.

Step three: Use this log as a deliver of motivation and terrific reinforcement.

2. Guided Visualization:

Step 1: Find a quiet vicinity and near your eye.

Step 2: Visualize a scenario where you correctly check your new patterns.

Step three: Feel the powerful feelings and sensations associated with that fulfillment. Repeat this visualization often to reinforce integration.

three. Self-Appreciation Letters:

Step 1: Write letters of appreciation to yourself acknowledging your achievements and development in imposing the modern day styles.

Step 2: Read those letters on the same time as you need a reminder of your potential for change and improvement.

4. Belief Reinforcement Exercises:

Step 1: Identify a terrific notion associated with your new idea sample.

Step 2: Perform reinforcement physical sports, which include repeating extremely good affirmations that assist this belief.

Step 3: Do this frequently to consolidate the ultra-current notion.

five. Repetition of Key Behaviors:

Step 1: Identify key behaviors related to your new styles.

Step 2: Set reminders and determine to consciously appearing those behaviors until they turn out to be automatic.

6. Practice in Real Scenarios:

Step 1: Find actual-life situations in which you could look at your new styles.

Step 2: Actively exercise those patterns in everyday conditions and check how they have an effect on your results.

7. Share Your Successes:

Step 1: Share your achievements and successes related to the aggregate of recent styles with pals or family.

Step 2: By sharing, you deliver a lift to your dedication and can get preserve of resource and congratulations that improve your motivation.

8. Continuous Review and Adjustment:

Step 1: Regularly assessment your dreams and the styles you need to combine.

Step 2: Make adjustments as critical based on your reviews and effects.

9. Self-Assessment of Progress:

Step 1: Establish a self-evaluation machine to degree your progress in integration.

Step 2: Use scales or signs and signs and symptoms to quantify your development and modify your approach in regions that want greater art work.

10. External Feedback:

Step 1: Seek optimistic feedback from relied on friends or mentors.

Step 2: Use the outside mind-set to discover regions wherein you could improve integration.

These sporting activities will assist you effectively integrate new belief and behavior styles into your every day life. Remember that steady exercising and dedication are key to reaching lasting and effective integration.

7.2. Strategies for Maintaining Long-Term Transformation

Maintaining prolonged-term transformation is as important as accomplishing it to begin with. Here are powerful strategies to ensure that the changes you have got implemented are sustained:

Set Clear and Meaningful Goals

To keep prolonged-time period transformation, having easy and great goals is crucial. These goals need to align along with your private values and aspirations. Define particular, measurable dreams that provide you with a clean direction.

Practice Continuous Self-Reflection

Regularly devote time to self-mirrored photograph. Examine your thoughts, feelings, and behaviors to make sure they may be consistent with your transformation dreams.

Self-mirrored image allows you keep consciousness of your improvement and come across capability deviations.

Build a Support System

Surrounding your self with a sturdy guide device is essential. Share your goals and traumatic conditions with pals, own family, or a relied on NLP therapist. Feedback and manual from others may be critical for retaining motivation and backbone.

Implement a Maintenance Plan

Develop a protection plan that includes every day practices and behavior that pork up new concept and conduct patterns. This might also moreover embody affirmations, visualization sports activities sports, and top notch techniques you have got determined effective.

Celebrate Small and Large Achievements

Acknowledge and feature an excellent time your achievements, whether small or huge.

Celebrations deliver a boost to the texture of achievement and encourage to hold moving in advance. This moreover facilitates hold a pleasing mind-set.

Avoid Complacency

Complacency may be an impediment to long-time period safety. Maintain an thoughts-set of non-stop improvement and avoid falling into routine or self-satisfaction. Being open to evolution will assist you develop continually.

Chapter 8: Practical Examples

In the previous chapters, we embarked on an exploratory journey thru the fascinating worldwide of Neuro Linguistic Programming (NLP). We unraveled the essential requirements and strategies that make up this powerful device for change and personal development. Now, it is time to location into workout what we've determined out and experiences firsthand the transformative impact of NLP.

In this chapter, we are able to awareness on tangible examples that illustrate the manner to exercise the techniques in the cloth of our everyday lives. The goal is to provide you with practical and usable tools that you may effortlessly combine into your every day habitual from enhancing interpersonal verbal exchange, dealing with pressure correctly, to refining your selection-making machine.

Although inside the course of this ebook I actually have already furnished numerous examples and physical activities, I need to offer you a similarly compendium that permits you to check, consolidate, and increase your expertise and talents in NLP. Below, you can find sports activities, each determined thru focused step-by the usage of-step commands. These bodily sports were designed to cope with a numerous kind of not unusual situations and challenges, providing progressive and effective solutions.

I am satisfied that steady and aware exercise is the critical aspect to internalizing the strategies and unleashing their transformative ability. So, I invite you to dive into the ones bodily activities with an open mind and a inclined coronary coronary coronary heart. As you exercise, reflect, and regulate your method, you may discover new views and strategies which will beautify your lifestyles revel in.

eight.1 Improvement of Communication

1. Conscious Body Language

Step 1: Choose an normal verbal exchange with a person.

Step 2: Focus to your frame language, which includes posture and gestures.

Step 3: Engage in a conscious communique, adjusting your body language to deliver self assurance and openness.

2. Empathy Reinforcement

Reverse Role-Playing Exercise

Objective: Foster the ability for empathy by means of using assuming the placement of the other character in a managed scenari.

Step 1: Role Selection

With a associate, select a current-day or hypothetical state of affairs in which every of you has professional or should experience high-quality or conflicting emotions.

Agree on who will assume the position of the possibility at some stage in the workout.

Step 2: Preparation

Each of you must describe to the alternative your actual (or capability, if it's miles a hypothetical situation) mind and feelings related to that scenario. Take notes if vital to don't forget crucial statistics.

Step 3: Role Immersion

Switch roles: fully anticipate the persona, posture, tone of voice, and emotional expressions of the opportunity as defined to you.

Step 4: Staging

Act out the scenario, reacting and responding due to the fact the opportunity character may additionally primarily based on the preceding description. Try to deeply apprehend how the opportunity feels, what motivates them, and what their problems are.

Step five: Dialogue and Discovery

During or after the enactment, communicate what each of you felt while assuming the function of the alternative. Was it difficult or clean? What factors have been the most difficult to empathize with?

Step 6: Joint Reflection

Reflect collectively on what changed into located. What did the exercise display screen approximately the other character's mindset? How can you use this new understanding to enhance verbal exchange and mutual assist in actual situations?

Conclusion:

This opposite characteristic-gambling workout allows participants to discover and immediately revel in the views and feelings of the alternative, promoting a deeper expertise and further empathy. By placing themselves inside the exceptional's footwear, it allows the identification and knowledge of emotions and motivations that may not have been glaring in advance than the workout.

3. Improvement of Vocal Intonation

Step 1: Record your voice whilst talking about a topic.

Step 2: Listen to the recording and compare your intonation.

Step 3: Practice various your intonation to supply messages extra in reality and emotionally.

8.2 Stress and Anxiety Management

four. Four-7-eight Breathing Technique

Step 1: Sit in a snug characteristic.

Step 2: Inhale through your nostril for 4 seconds.

Step three: Hold your breath for 7 seconds.

Step four: Exhale without a doubt over eight seconds.

Step 5: Repeat this cycle for severa minutes to reduce strain.

5. Visualization of a Tranquil Place

Step 1: Close your eyes and take deep breaths.

Step 2: Visualize a non violent and relaxing location, which includes a seashore or a woodland.

Step three: Immerse yourself inside the intellectual photograph, feeling the peace and relaxation.

eight.Three Improvement of Decision Making

6. Pros and Cons List Process

Step 1: Write down a choice you need to make.

Step 2: Create lists, one for execs and any other for cons for every opportunity.

Step 3: Evaluate the lists and make a choice based totally truely on the records.

7. Modeling Leadership Skills

Objective: Develop control and effective communique abilties via searching at and emulating the traits of an awesome leader.

Step 1: Leader Selection

Select a pacesetter in your trouble of hobby or in some different vicinity whom you admire for their management and verbal exchange skills. This may be someone you apprehend in my view, a ancient chief, a public parent, or maybe a fictional man or woman recognized for their management talents.

Step 2: Research and Analysis

Research this leader. Read about their lifestyles, watch films in their speeches or interviews, and look at their interactions with others. Pay precise hobby to how they communicate their thoughts, how they encourage others, and the manner they cope with difficult conditions.

Step 3: Breakdown of Skills

List the right verbal exchange and leadership talents this person possesses. This may additionally need to include their functionality to pay attention, their eloquence in talking, their manner of giving advantageous comments, how they inspire self assurance, among exclusive dispositions.

Step 4: Practice Specific Skills

Choose a specific expertise you want to expand. For instance, if you have determined on a leader for his or her potential to encourage their institution, you might attention on how they use motivational language.

Create hypothetical situations or characteristic-performs in which you can practice this skills. For example, you could simulate a assembly in which you need to inspire your institution inside the face of a task.

Step 5: Feedback and Continuous Improvement

Practice the capacity in low-hazard actual-existence situations to achieve feedback. This may be in small meetings, one-on-one conversations, or perhaps in providing a undertaking.

Analyze the reactions of humans and ask for direct remarks for your normal overall performance. Use this records to regulate and decorate your technique.

Step 6: Integration of Skills

Gradually integrate extra talents from your function model into your management repertoire. Don't restrict yourself to imitation; adapt the skills in your character and context to lead them to real.

Step 7: Personal Reflection and Adjustments

After each attempt to observe those competencies, take a 2d to mirror at the approach. What worked nicely? What may be stepped forward?

Adjust your behavior primarily based in reality for your reflections and the feedback obtained to continuously first-rate your management style.

Conclusion:

This workout permits you construct a difficult and fast of manage and conversation competencies by using looking at and emulating the characteristics of an effective leader. By applying those capabilities on your non-public and professional existence, you could boom your own management fashion caused through the outstanding practices of someone you apprehend.

eight.Four Changing Limiting Beliefs

8. Reframing via Therapeutic Writing

Objective: Transform restricting ideals into empowering beliefs through mirrored image and personal writing.

Step 1: Writing for Identification

Take a bit of paper or open a report to your laptop and write down the limiting notion you need to alternate. Describe how this belief affects you to your each day lifestyles and in attaining your dreams.

Step 2: Analysis of Origin

Reflect and write approximately the inspiration of this perception. When did you begin believing this? What stories reinforced it? How has this perception advanced over time?

Step 3: Critical Questioning

Challenge the validity of this notion with powerful questions. Write down as a minimum three portions of proof or opinions that show that this perception may not be completely real or that there are times whilst it does now not look at.

Step four: Search for Alternatives

Write a list of opportunity beliefs that might be more beneficial and superb. These need to not be idealized or unrealistic, but positive and based totally to your real talents.

Step 5: Building Arguments

For every new empowering notion, draft a stable argument about why it's miles a greater realistic and beneficial opportunity to the appropriate proscribing belief.

Step 6: Creation of Affirmations

Transform those opportunity beliefs into wonderful affirmations. For example, in case your limiting belief is "I am not excellent in public," an empowering confirmation may be "Each time I revel in greater comfortable and assured speakme in public".

Step 7: Daily Integration

Commit to studying and reflecting on the ones affirmations each morning and each night time. You can keep a mag of your development and the way those new ideals are helping you change your conduct and memories.

Step eight: Celebrating Successes

Each time you act according together together with your new empowering ideals, take a 2nd to have amusing it and write it down. This reinforces the cutting-edge belief and its electricity on your life.

Conclusion:

This workout of reframing thru recuperation writing lets in you to artwork deeply on transforming your proscribing ideals. The machine of writing, studying, and reformulating permits to make clear your thoughts and deliver a boost to new, extra advantageous perspectives.

eight.Five Enhancement of Creativity

nine. Visual Brainstorming

Step 1: Choose a subject or problem.

Step 2: Draw a primary photograph representing the challenge in the middle of a bit of paper.

Step 3: Draw branches extending from the crucial photograph and add related visual thoughts.

10. Creative Word Association

Step 1: Choose a random word or concern count number.

Step 2: Associate related words or ideas, developing a series of associations.

Step 3: Use the ones institutions to encourage you in innovative duties.

11. Collaborative Story Writing

Step 1: Collaborate with a person else to write down a brief tale.

Step 2: Take turns writing paragraphs or sections of the story, maintaining the creativity flowing.

12. Clay Sculpting

Step 1: Get a few clay and begin shaping a determine without a specific plan in thoughts.

Step 2: Let your instinct and creativity guide the approach.

8.6 Improvement of Self-Esteem

thirteen. "Personal Timeline" for Self-Esteem

Objective: Create a seen illustration of your private boom and achievements to reinforce self-worth and conceitedness.

Step 1: Creation of Your Timeline

Use a huge sheet of paper or a board and draw a line representing your lifestyles from start to the modern. Mark giant years or intervals.

Step 2: Identification of Positive Milestones

Reflect on the happiest moments and achievements of your lifestyles. These can consist of private small victories, overcoming boundaries, reached desires, friendships formed, abilties located, and many others.

Step three: Visual Representation of Achievements

Place the ones moments along the timeline with drawings, images, clippings, or notes. Each need to have a brief description of what occurred and why it's far essential to you.

Step 4: Emotional Connection with the Events

As you place each event, take a 2d to bear in thoughts how you felt at that point. Relive the sensation of pride, pleasure, or gratitude related to each success.

Step 5: Reflection on the Lessons Learned

For every milestone, write next to it a lesson you observed or a energy you determined in yourself way to that experience.

Step 6: Recognition of Personal Evolution

Once completed, take time to take a look at your complete timeline. Observe how each occasion has led you to be the character you're in recent times. Consciously apprehend your evolution and private growth.

Step 7: Celebration and Commitment

Celebrate this journey that is your life. Commit to keep together with extraordinary moments on your timeline, recognizing that every day you have got the possibility to create new achievements and getting to know.

Conclusion:

This exercising permits you to visualise your development and strengths in a tangible way, fostering a more appreciation on your existence adventure and the competencies you have got were given advanced. It's a visual and emotional reminder that each enjoy has contributed on your growth and that you are worth of esteem and apprehend.

14. Three-Step Self-Compassion

Objective: Develop an thoughts-set of self-compassion and kindness within the route of oneself, critical for healthy vanity.

Step 1: Positive Inner Dialogue

Start the day thru putting in a pleasing inner speak. In the the the front of the replicate, make sensible and unique high-quality affirmations about yourself. For example, in location of pronouncing "I am the first-rate," you can say "Today I will use my creativity to resolve the annoying conditions that upward thrust up".

Step 2: Personal Kindness Act

During the day, perform at least one act of kindness closer to yourself. This can be taking a 2nd to experience an hobby you want, treating your self to a few thing small that makes you glad, or truely giving your self permission to rest in case you want it.

Step three: Nighttime Self-Compassion Reflection

At the surrender of the day, take a few minutes to mirror at the manner you dealt with your self. Write in a mag the techniques in which you were type to yourself and how you felt about it. If there had been moments at the same time as you were crucial of your self, replicate on how you can cope with your self with extra compassion in the future.

Step four: Gratitude for Self

Also write down 3 subjects approximately your self for which you are grateful. They can be attributes of your personality, achievements of the day, or sincerely popularity of your each day strive.

Step five: Commitment to Continuous Improvement

Before going to sleep, determine to enhancing in a particular location the next day, however from an area of compassion, not grievance. For example, "Tomorrow I will maintain schooling staying power with myself at the same time as reading a few component new, information that it is ok to make mistakes".

Conclusion:

This self-compassion exercise lets in you assemble a kinder and greater facts relationship with your self. By recognizing and celebrating your efforts and trends, and through lightly addressing your areas for development, you may boom your arrogance and emotional well-being.

8.7 Development of Social Skills

15. Communication Role-Playing Game

Step 1: Act out hard communique situations, together with handing over horrific facts or coping with conflicts, in a function-playing game with a chum.

Step 2: Practice particular strategies and communication strategies.

sixteen. "Round Table" for Social Skills Development

Objective: Promote the development of verbal exchange competencies, argumentation, and active listening in an concept-change surroundings.

Step 1: Setting the Stage

Organize a hard and fast of buddies or buddies interested by enhancing their social capabilities. Create an surroundings much like a "round table" in which everybody can see and pay attention each exceptional.

Step 2: Selection of Topics

Write specific brand new hobby topics on small papers. These can be contemporary troubles, moral dilemmas, or hypothetical conditions that require innovative answers.

Step 3: Speaking Turns

Each individual alternatives a paper and is given a limited time, for example, 5 minutes, to provide their factor of view at the assigned subject matter. The others ought to pay interest without interrupting.

Chapter 9: Nlp For Personal Development

Setting and Achieving Goals with NLP

In the world of private development, enterprise agency success, sports activities sports activities overall performance enhancement and numerous distinctive areas of lifestyles, putting and achieving desires is a critical detail of increase and development. Neuro Linguistic Programming (NLP) offers effective machine and strategies that would substantially help individuals in this approach. By harnessing the strength of the mind and information the connection among language, mind, and behavior, NLP gives a very unique approach to goal putting and attainment.

NLP emphasizes the importance of readability in terms of setting dreams. Without a clear and unique intention, it turns into hard to direct our awareness and rent our resources efficaciously. By using NLP techniques such as visualization and reframing, human beings can benefit a crystal-easy know-how of what they clearly preference and create compelling goals that ignite their motivation.

One of the middle ideas of NLP is the idea that our mind and ideals shape our reality. By figuring out and transforming limiting beliefs, we will put off self-imposed limitations that keep away from our improvement. NLP strategies like notion exchange styles and anchoring can assist human beings rewire their mindset, permitting them to conquer limitations and obtain their desires with greater ease.

Furthermore, NLP presents strategies for powerful cause planning and implementation. Techniques much like the nicely-customary final results and the NLP goal-placing approach permit humans to break down their goals into possible steps, growing a roadmap for success. Additionally, through making use of NLP techniques which include modeling and mirroring, people can studies from the achievements of others and reflect their success strategies.

NLP additionally offers powerful equipment for preserving motivation and overcoming setbacks. By the use of techniques similar to the clean pattern and the circle of excellence, people can enhance their self assurance, overcome procrastination, and stay focused on their desires. Moreover, NLP strategies for handling stress and anxiety, collectively with the short phobia remedy and the timeline approach, can assist humans conquer traumatic conditions and live resilient inside the face of barriers.

In end, placing and undertaking desires with NLP is a transformative manner that would result in non-public, professional, and famous lifestyles transformation. By utilizing the powerful strategies and strategies supplied through NLP, people can gain clarity, redesign their thoughts-set, create effective plans, and conquer boundaries on their route to fulfillment. Whether it is personal development, employer and management, sports activities activities ordinary universal overall performance enhancement, or each unique place of existence, incorporating NLP into intention putting and attainment can loose up untapped capability and open doors to new opportunities.

Enhancing Self-Confidence and Self-Esteem

Self-self perception and arrogance are critical inclinations that would drastically impact our non-public and expert lives. In this subchapter, we're capable of find out how Neuro Linguistic Programming (NLP) may be used to beautify those developments, allowing people from all walks of existence to launch their entire functionality.

NLP techniques offer powerful equipment for individuals looking for non-public improvement, superior verbal exchange skills, and extended self-assure. By understanding how our mind, language, and behavior are interconnected, NLP empowers us to make great changes in our lives.

For those in commercial organization and control roles, self-self warranty is essential for making powerful options, inspiring groups, and achieving achievement. NLP techniques can assist individuals overcome proscribing ideals, increase a winning mindset, and enhance their communication abilties to end up influential leaders.

Athletes and performers can also benefit from NLP to optimize their sports activities sports overall performance. By using techniques along with visualization, anchoring, and reframing, athletes can improve their self-self warranty, attention, and motivation, fundamental to advanced outcomes on the arena or degree.

Phobias and fears can regularly maintain us again from dwelling our lives to the fullest. NLP gives powerful strategies to triumph over those obstacles thru rewiring our idea patterns and changing worry with self assurance. Through strategies just like the Fast Phobia Cure, people can conquer their fears and regain manage over their lives.

In relationships and communique, self-self assurance and self-esteem play a important function. NLP provides realistic system to enhance rapport, active listening, and powerful conversation capabilities. By growing a deeper know-how of ourselves and others, we can assemble more potent and more enjoyable relationships.

The stresses of cutting-edge lifestyles can regularly cause tension and overwhelm. NLP techniques can help humans manage strain and reduce tension by using reframing bad mind, anchoring splendid feelings, and utilizing relaxation strategies. With prolonged self-self perception and arrogance, individuals can face worrying conditions with resilience and tranquility.

Public speakme and presentation competencies are crucial in hundreds of expert settings. NLP gives techniques to triumph over stage fright, enhance shipping, and hook up with the intention market on a deeper degree. By improving self-self notion and vanity, humans can deliver impactful shows without difficulty.

NLP also offers strategies to improve memory and reading abilities. By making use of visualization, affiliation, and using sensory structures, humans can decorate their reminiscence keep in mind and accelerate their studying technique.

For the ones looking to gain a extra healthy way of life, NLP may be accomplished to weight loss and commonplace nicely-being. By addressing the underlying ideals and behaviors that make a contribution to risky behavior, human beings can expand more healthy behavior, beautify self-self guarantee, and benefit their weight loss goals.

Finally, NLP can foster creativity and innovation through breaking thru proscribing ideals and growing our questioning styles. By utilizing techniques like reframing, human beings can shift their views and unfastened up their revolutionary functionality.

In end, enhancing self-confidence and conceitedness is important for non-public growth and achievement in numerous components of existence. Through the effective strategies of NLP, people can triumph over limiting ideals, triumph over fears, beautify communication competencies, manage strain, improve normal typical performance, and advantage their desires. Whether you're trying to find private development, expert growth, or superior relationships, NLP gives a comprehensive toolkit to disencumber your whole capability.

Overcoming Limiting Beliefs and Negative Thought Patterns

In our journey in the direction of private boom and achievement, simply considered one of the largest limitations we're dealing with is our own proscribing beliefs and terrible concept patterns. These self-imposed barriers keep us lower lower back from achieving our complete capability and avoid our ability to advantage our dreams.

However, with the energy of Neuro Linguistic Programming (NLP), we are capable of harm unfastened from these constraints and create the existence we genuinely choice.

Limiting beliefs are deeply ingrained thoughts and convictions that restriction us from exploring new opportunities. They are frequently fashioned via past reports, societal conditioning, or horrible self-talk. These beliefs act as a barrier, preventing us from stepping out of our comfort region and taking dangers. However, NLP strategies can assist us challenge and reprogram the ones ideals, allowing us to redefine our competencies and enlarge our horizons.

Negative belief styles, but, are habitual thoughts that generate feelings of self-doubt, worry, or tension. They can sabotage our efforts and save you us from taking motion. NLP gives powerful device to find out and transform the ones idea patterns into immoderate fantastic, empowering ones. By replacing terrible thoughts with excessive fantastic affirmations and visualizations, we're capable of alternate our mind-set and domesticate a extra positive outlook on existence.

NLP techniques are applicable to numerous regions of our lives, on the side of private development, commercial enterprise and control, sports sports regular performance enhancement, overcoming phobias and fears, relationship and verbal exchange abilties, strain manipulate and tension cut price, public speakme and presentation skills, improving reminiscence and analyzing abilties, weight loss and wholesome life-style, further to creativity and innovation enhancement.

By analyzing NLP, we are capable to conquer our proscribing beliefs and bad idea patterns, allowing us to free up our actual functionality in a number of these regions. Whether we want to excel in our expert lives, enhance our private relationships, or beautify our physical and highbrow nicely-being, NLP offers a holistic approach to self-development.

In "Mastering Your Mind: The Ultimate Guide to Neuro Linguistic Programming," you'll discover sensible NLP strategies and carrying sports specifically designed to deal with those limiting ideals and terrible idea patterns. Through step-through-step instructions, real-life examples, and case studies, you'll learn how to rewire your mind for success and create lasting alternate in all regions of your life.

No rely in which you're for your adventure, it is never too past due to overcome your proscribing ideals and awful concept patterns. With the strength of NLP, you may redecorate your attitude and create the existence you have were given always dreamed of. So, dive into the sector of NLP and unleash your whole potential these days!

Developing Effective Communication Skills

Effective communication is a essential factor of human interaction, and gaining knowledge of it could significantly beautify different factors of our lives. Whether you are trying to improve your private relationships, excel in business company and manage, decorate your sports sports common performance, triumph over fears and phobias, manage pressure and tension, supply impactful suggests, enhance reminiscence and reading talents, benefit weight reduction and a healthy manner of lifestyles, or foster creativity and innovation, growing powerful verbal exchange competencies via Neuro Linguistic Programming (NLP) can be the crucial element for your fulfillment.

NLP gives a effective set of strategies and techniques which can remodel the manner you communicate with others and yourself. By understanding how language and behavior have an effect on our thoughts and emotions, NLP gives device to enlarge rapport, construct receive as actual with, and impact others really. Whether you are a beginner or an professional practitioner, analyzing effective verbal exchange skills thru NLP can significantly effect your non-public and expert existence.

In non-public relationships, effective communique is critical for developing sturdy connections and resolving conflicts. NLP strategies let you increase empathy, active listening, and powerful wondering skills. By expertise and using non-verbal communication cues, which includes frame language and tonality, NLP can beautify your functionality to recognize and connect with others on a deeper degree.

In the economic business enterprise and management realm, effective communique is important for motivating and frightening agencies, negotiating deals, and constructing a fulfillment relationships with customers and stakeholders. NLP can equip you with influential language styles, persuasive strategies, and rapport-building techniques to come to be a charismatic leader and gather your desires.

For sports activities activities sports activities overall performance enhancement, NLP offers strategies to overcome highbrow blocks, growth self assurance, and enhance consciousness. By using visualization, anchoring, and goal-putting techniques, athletes can decorate their simple overall performance and collect top states of thoughts.

NLP can also facilitate overcoming fears and phobias with the aid of using rewiring terrible perception patterns and converting them with superb ones. Through strategies which encompass the glossy sample and timeline treatment, NLP can help people reframe their perceptions and triumph over their fears.

In the place of pressure control and anxiety reduce rate, NLP offers system to reprogram the thoughts, manage emotions, and adopt empowering ideals. By utilizing strategies which includes the circle of excellence and anchoring, people can reap a rustic of calmness and resilience.

For public talking and presentation abilties, NLP techniques can help people triumph over degree fright, supply impactful speeches, and engage their target market effectively. By expertise the energy of language and using strategies in conjunction with pacing and leading, people can become assured and persuasive audio gadget.

NLP moreover offers techniques to beautify memory and studying talents. By utilizing visualization, association, and chunking techniques, people can decorate their functionality to go through in mind and don't forget data efficaciously.

In the place of weight reduction and a healthy way of life, NLP can assist humans reprogram their dating with meals, overcome cravings, and adopt empowering behavior. By using techniques consisting of reframing and anchoring, people can boom a first rate mind-set inside the path of their health and well-being.

Lastly, NLP strategies can foster creativity and innovation through manner of unlocking the unconscious thoughts and stimulating new mind. By using techniques collectively with brainstorming and reframing, people can growth their wondering and unleash their innovative functionality.

In end, developing effective conversation capabilities through NLP may additionally want to have a profound impact on different factors of our lives. Whether you're looking for private increase, professional success, or advanced properly-being, NLP offers a flexible set of strategies and techniques that will help you come to be a hold close communicator. By records and utilizing the strength of language and behavior, you may create excessive best trade, overcome limitations, and advantage your desired outcomes.

Chapter 10: Nlp For Business And Leadership

Building Rapport and Influencing Others

In the arena of Neuro Linguistic Programming (NLP), building rapport and influencing others is a fundamental understanding that may be completed to a huge variety of regions, which consist of private development, corporation and manage, sports activities activities performance enhancement, overcoming phobias and fears, dating and verbal exchange abilties, strain control and anxiety discount, public talking and presentation abilities, improving memory and studying abilities, weight reduction and healthy way of life, further to creativity and innovation enhancement.

Rapport is the inspiration of powerful communique and connection. It is the functionality to installation a harmonious and trusting dating with others, taking into account open and receptive communique. When we have had been given rapport, the effect we have over others will increase exponentially, permitting us to achieve our desired results extra with out difficulty.

One of the middle principles of NLP is the know-how that people have terrific communique styles and opportunities. By becoming aware about these person variations, we're able to adapt our verbal exchange to healthy that of others, thereby constructing rapport outcomes. This capacity to comply is known as pacing and fundamental.

Pacing involves mirroring and matching the other person's non-verbal conduct, which consist of their frame language, tone of voice, and respiratory styles. By subtly aligning ourselves with the possibility person, we create a sense of familiarity and similarity, which fosters believe and connection. Once rapport has been set up through pacing, we are able to then lead the interplay with the aid of introducing our private communication style and thoughts.

Influencing others is an quintessential part of ordinary life, whether or not or not or no longer it is persuading a customer to buy a product, motivating personnel to gain their desires, or inspiring a accomplice to undertake extra wholesome behavior. NLP gives a variety of techniques to enhance our capability to persuade others truely.

One such approach is the use of language patterns. By cautiously choosing and structuring our phrases, we will elicit precise responses and form the wondering and behavior of others. NLP moreover emphasizes the significance of know-how and utilizing the energy of our subconscious thoughts. By gaining access to and speaking with the unconscious, we are able to skip resistance and create lasting trade in ourselves and others.

In end, building rapport and influencing others is a crucial functionality in diverse elements of existence, from private improvement to industrial employer and control, sports sports performance enhancement to overcoming fears and phobias. Through the standards and techniques of NLP, we're capable of grasp the art work of rapport constructing, allowing us to attach deeply with others and have an effect on them definitely. By making use of these competencies, we will decorate our relationships, gather our desires, and create a more appealing and successful existence.

Effective Negotiation and Persuasion Techniques

Whether you are aiming to excel in personal development, enterprise and manipulate, sports sports activities general overall performance enhancement, overcoming fears and phobias, improving relationships and communique capabilities, handling stress and tension, public speakme and presentation, improving memory and analyzing competencies, attaining weight loss and a healthy way of existence, or boosting creativity and innovation, gaining knowledge of the art work of negotiation and persuasion is a crucial potential to personal. In this subchapter, we are capable of delve into the area of powerful negotiation and persuasion strategies, and find out how Neuro Linguistic Programming (NLP) may be executed to beautify your talents in those regions.

Negotiation is an inherent part of our each day lives, from making alternatives with our loved ones to ultimate business business enterprise gives. To grow to be a successful negotiator, it's miles important to recognize the requirements of effective communication, rapport building, and persuasive language patterns. NLP affords a valuable framework for honing the ones skills.

One of the crucial thing strategies in negotiation is to increase rapport with the alternative birthday party. NLP gives severa techniques to installation rapport quickly, which encompass mirroring body language, matching tonality, and pacing the alternative person's language patterns. By building a revel in of believe and connection, you could create an surroundings conducive to a fulfillment negotiation.

Persuasion, alternatively, involves influencing others to adopt your standpoint or take a preferred path of movement. NLP equips you with quite a few persuasive language styles, at the side of embedded commands, presuppositions, and analogical reasoning. These strategies allow you to speak with effect, have interaction the subconscious mind, and evoke favored responses.

Additionally, NLP allow you to discover and triumph over any proscribing beliefs or bad emotions that might save you your negotiation and persuasion abilties. By the use of strategies like timeline remedy and reframing, you could do away with self-doubt, growth self belief, and loose up your full potential.

Whether you're negotiating a company deal, motivating a crew, or seeking out to conquer non-public limitations, analyzing the art work of negotiation and persuasion thru NLP strategies will extensively beautify your possibilities of achievement. By records the ideas of effective communication, constructing rapport, and the usage of persuasive language patterns, you may come to be a extra influential and persuasive communicator in any area of your lifestyles.

In end, this subchapter on powerful negotiation and persuasion techniques pastimes to provide treasured insights and realistic techniques for individuals interested by private development, business organisation and management, sports activities common overall performance enhancement, overcoming fears and phobias, enhancing relationships and conversation abilties, managing stress and tension, public talking and presentation, enhancing reminiscence and getting to know talents, accomplishing weight reduction and a healthy way of life, and boosting creativity and innovation. By using the concepts of NLP, you may refine your negotiation and persuasion competencies, fundamental to extra achievement and success in all regions of your lifestyles.

Leadership Development thru NLP

In extremely-current rapid-paced and aggressive international, effective management talents are essential for fulfillment in numerous regions of lifestyles. Whether you aspire to be a business chief, excel in sports activities, construct healthful relationships, or in reality beautify your private development, learning the artwork of manipulate is essential. This subchapter explores how Neuro Linguistic Programming (NLP) can be a effective device for growing incredible control skills.

NLP, a innovative approach to statistics human conduct and communique, offers a range of strategies and strategies that might assist humans release their capability and become influential leaders. By adopting NLP thoughts, people can make bigger a deep know-how of themselves and others, decorate conversation talents, and gain the capability to encourage and inspire the ones round them.

In the commercial enterprise world, powerful control is critical for the usage of growth, dealing with organizations, and engaging in organizational desires. NLP strategies which consist of modeling a hit leaders, mastering non-verbal conversation, and knowledge the energy of language can considerably enhance manipulate abilities. By applying NLP in a commercial enterprise enterprise context, human beings can build sturdy relationships with team human beings, manage conflicts correctly, and create a first-rate and efficient paintings surroundings.

NLP additionally can be immensely beneficial for sports activities activities sports overall performance enhancement. By utilizing strategies like visualization, anchoring, and purpose placing, athletes can beautify their reputation, enhance self assure, and maximize their ability. NLP permits athletes overcome fears, manage stress and anxiety, and growth a prevailing mind-set, ultimately essential to progressed standard performance on the sector or court docket.

In the realm of private development, NLP gives numerous gear for overcoming phobias and fears, improving communique abilities, reducing strain and anxiety, improving reminiscence and learning abilities, or even achieving weight reduction and a wholesome manner of existence. NLP strategies at the side of reframing terrible beliefs, the use of language patterns effectively, and getting access to creative states can empower people to conquer limitations, set and benefit dreams, and lead a satisfying existence.

Furthermore, NLP can extensively advantage human beings searching out to beautify their creativity and innovation. By knowledge the form of creativity, using techniques like brainstorming and sample interrupt, and learning to expect outside the sphere, human beings can tap into their modern functionality and generate modern thoughts.

Overall, whether or no longer or now not you're in search of to end up a better leader, decorate your sports sports universal overall performance, beautify your private improvement, or gain fulfillment in various areas of existence, NLP offers a powerful framework for control development. By incorporating NLP techniques and strategies into your every day life, you may loose up your entire capability, inspire the ones around you, and grow to be a fairly powerful and influential leader.

Enhancing Presentation and Public Speaking Skills

Effective presentation and public speakme abilties are vital in various components of lifestyles, from private improvement to enterprise company and management, sports sports performance enhancement to overcoming phobias and fears. Whether you're seeking to enhance your conversation competencies, reduce tension, or beautify your memory and getting to know skills, mastering the artwork of public speakme can be transformative.

Neuro Linguistic Programming (NLP) gives powerful strategies to assist people excel in supplying their mind, charming their target market, and conveying their message with self notion and effect. In this subchapter, we are able to explore how NLP may be applied to beautify presentation and public speaking abilties at some point of unique niches.

For those pursuing personal improvement, NLP offers techniques to overcome restricting ideals and raise self-self perception. By utilising techniques inclusive of anchoring and reframing, people can rewire their mind to encompass extremely good thoughts and overcome degree fright.

In the world of employer and management, effective verbal exchange is vital. NLP strategies collectively with rapport building, mirroring, and matching can help installation a reference to the audience, fostering accept as true with and credibility. Additionally, the usage of language styles and persuasive strategies can beautify the ability to influence and convince others.

Sports regular usual overall performance enhancement can appreciably advantage from NLP techniques for presentation and public speaking. By the use of visualization and intellectual exercise consultation, athletes can decorate their pre-recreation speeches, interviews, and motivational talks, essential to advanced usual overall performance and highbrow resilience.

NLP can also be instrumental in overcoming phobias and fears associated with public talking. Through strategies just like the Fast Phobia Cure, humans can reframe their notion of speakme in public, decreasing anxiety and permitting them to present honestly and self notion.

In the vicinity of relationship and conversation talents, NLP offers precious gear for effective public speaking. By information the power of language styles, body language, and tonality, human beings can speak their thoughts and feelings greater efficaciously, fostering healthier and extra widespread connections.

Furthermore, NLP techniques for pressure manipulate and anxiety cut price can be carried out to public speakme contexts. By utilising strategies like anchoring and timeline treatment, human beings can manage their pressure tiers and input a kingdom of height standard overall performance, taking into consideration extra impactful displays.

Chapter 11: Nlp For Sports Performance Enhancement

Mental Preparation for Sports Success

In the arena of sports activities, physical training and skill development are often the primary cognizance for athletes. However, what many fail to apprehend is that highbrow practise plays a important role in attaining fulfillment on the field, court docket, or song. This subchapter will delve into the significance of intellectual steering for sports activities sports success and the manner Neuro Linguistic Programming (NLP) may be applied to decorate overall performance.

Athletes in any respect stages can gain from making use of NLP strategies to optimize their thoughts-set in advance than competition. NLP for sports activities sports activities ordinary overall performance enhancement focuses on harnessing the power of the mind to enhance cognizance, enhance self warranty, and enhance everyday overall overall performance.

One key component of intellectual training is visualization. By the usage of NLP strategies which includes guided imagery, athletes can mentally rehearse their ordinary performance, envisioning each pass, approach, and outcome. This exercising lets in to create a intellectual blueprint for success, permitting athletes to carry out at their high-quality even because it subjects most.

Another crucial element of highbrow education is handling anxiety and strain. NLP for stress control and tension reduction gives athletes with effective tools to calm their nerves and stay composed underneath strain. Techniques at the side of anchoring, wherein a amazing emotion or state is related to a physical gesture or motive, can be used to brief shift from tension to a confident and targeted u . S ..

Furthermore, NLP for reinforcing memory and getting to know abilities can resource athletes in absorbing and keeping records essential to their overall performance. By the usage of techniques on the facet of the "chunking" technique, athletes can harm down complex competencies or plays into smaller, extra workable factors. This allows for easier learning and improved bear in mind at some stage in competition.

Effective verbal exchange and building sturdy relationships are also vital in sports sports. NLP for relationship and verbal exchange abilities can help athletes expand rapport with teammates, coaches, and fighters. By expertise and the usage of non-verbal cues, body language, and powerful language styles, athletes can decorate their capacity to hook up with others, fostering a collaborative and supportive surroundings.

Lastly, NLP for non-public development and goal placing can help athletes in placing clean desires and growing a roadmap for conducting them. By utilizing NLP strategies which include the well-formed final results, athletes can define their dreams in a way that maximizes motivation and continues them heading inside the proper direction for achievement.

In give up, mental education is a important factor of sports activities achievement. By incorporating NLP techniques into their education regimen, athletes can optimize their mind-set, decorate reputation, increase self perception, manage stress, enhance memory and gaining knowledge of abilties, foster sturdy relationships, and set and benefit goals. Whether you're a professional athlete, a weekend warrior, or a sports activities enthusiast, harnessing the energy of your thoughts thru NLP can unencumber your proper capacity and propel you closer to sports activities activities success.

Developing Focus and Concentration

In modern-day rapid-paced international, it could be difficult to stay targeted and preserve attention amidst the distractions and desires of ordinary life. Whether you're searching for non-public growth, professional fulfillment, or progressed performance in sports activities activities, growing interest and attention is essential. In this subchapter, we are capable of discover how Neuro Linguistic Programming (NLP) assist you to enhance your ability to pay interest and obtain your desires.

NLP strategies are designed to reprogram your thoughts, permitting you to faucet into your whole functionality. By knowledge the relationship among language, thoughts, and behavior, you may discover ways to direct your interest and increase laser-like focus. Here are some practical strategies to help you beautify your interest and hobby:

1. Anchoring: NLP teaches you the manner to create anchors, which may be effective triggers that can proper away convey you into a nation of cognizance. By associating a specific gesture or phrase with a centered u . S . A ., you can without problems get right of get admission to to that kingdom every time needed.

2. Visualizations: Visualization is a powerful tool in NLP. By vividly imagining your self in a focused state, you can educate your mind to stay gift and give interest to the assignment to be had. Visualizations assist you to get rid of distractions and live centered in your dreams.

3. Submodalities: NLP explores the sensory elements of our studies. By expertise and manipulating the submodalities of your thoughts, along with brightness, duration, and region, you may beautify your ability to pay attention. For example, making your highbrow pix brighter and closer can intensify your attention.

four. Eliminating Limiting Beliefs: NLP lets in you perceive and overcome limiting beliefs that can be hindering your functionality to pay interest. By changing terrible thoughts with brilliant affirmations, you may reprogram your mind for fulfillment and superior hobby.

five. Mindfulness Techniques: NLP emphasizes the significance of being fully present within the moment. Mindfulness techniques, together with deep respiration physical sports and meditation, will permit you to quiet your mind, reduce distractions, and decorate your cognizance.

Whether you're an athlete seeking out pinnacle universal performance, an entrepreneur aiming for employer success, or an man or woman looking to conquer fears and phobias, NLP gives a whole method to growing popularity and reputation. By applying the ones techniques for your each day existence, you may beautify your memory, decorate creativity, reduce stress, and reap your goals.

Remember, growing reputation and cognizance is a potential that may be determined and mastered through normal exercise. With NLP, you've got the machine to loose up your thoughts's capability and unharness your real capabilities. Start implementing the ones strategies these days and experience the transformation in your private and professional lifestyles.

Overcoming Performance Anxiety and Pressure

Performance tension and strain may be overwhelming, whether or no longer or not you are an athlete, a business leader, a pupil, or a person genuinely looking for to decorate their communication abilties. The fear of failure, the pressure to be triumphant, and the tension of being judged can restrict your functionality to carry out at your amazing. However, with the techniques and techniques of Neuro Linguistic Programming (NLP), you could triumph over those disturbing conditions and liberate your full capacity.

NLP offers diverse machine and strategies to help you manage and conquer common average overall performance anxiety and stress. By statistics how your thoughts works and studying to control your mind and emotions, you could construct resilience, beautify your self guarantee, and carry out at your peak.

One powerful approach is reframing, which includes converting the manner you apprehend a situation or revel in. By reframing your mind approximately performance tension and pressure, you could turn them into quality motivators in desire to terrible stumbling blocks. NLP additionally teaches you the manner to apply visualization and intellectual practice session to create a nice highbrow image of success, assisting to lessen anxiety and boom self assurance.

Another effective NLP method is anchoring, which entails associating a particular bodily or highbrow nation with a preferred emotion or conduct. By developing an anchor, which encompass a specific gesture or word, you may quick get proper of access to a country of calm and self notion on the same time as faced with trendy overall performance anxiety or stress. This technique lets in you to take control of your emotions and perform at your first rate, no matter the outside conditions.

In addition to these techniques, NLP offers pretty a number of conversation and rapport-constructing talents to be able to will let you navigate pressure-stuffed situations. By gaining knowledge of the artwork of effective communication, you could assemble sturdy relationships, manage conflicts, and encourage others, improving your not unusual overall performance in each private and expert settings.

Whether you're an athlete striving for peak regular performance, a commercial enterprise leader searching out to excel beneath pressure, or a person honestly trying to overcome their fear of public speakme, NLP gives realistic and confirmed techniques for achievement. By gaining knowledge of your thoughts via NLP, you can conquer usual overall performance anxiety and strain, release your complete ability, and gain your desires in any location of lifestyles. So, take the first step toward analyzing your thoughts and unleash the power of NLP to transform your general performance and life.

Enhancing Motivation and Confidence in Sports

Sports normal performance is not quite a good deal physical capabilities; it is also heavily encouraged by way of the use of highbrow electricity and attitude. To excel in sports activities activities, athletes ought to no longer simplest possess the essential skills and strategies but additionally have excessive motivation and unwavering self assurance. In this subchapter, we can find out how Neuro Linguistic Programming (NLP) can be finished to enhance motivation and self assurance in sports activities sports sports, reaping blessings people during numerous niches at the side of non-public development, organization and manipulate, and sports activities sports everyday standard performance enhancement.

NLP offers diverse techniques and strategies that might assist athletes obtain their complete potential. One such technique is visualization, wherein athletes create colorful highbrow images of themselves succeeding in their hobby. By over and over visualizing success, athletes can improve their self guarantee and motivation, as the thoughts becomes familiar with the feeling of accomplishment. NLP additionally emphasizes the power of incredible self-talk, encouraging athletes to replace self-doubt and negative thoughts with first rate affirmations and notion of their competencies. This shift in mind-set can drastically decorate motivation and self warranty, most critical to progressed sports sports sports common overall performance.

Additionally, NLP techniques like anchoring and reframing may be used to control and conquer fears and phobias that could keep away from an athlete's everyday general overall performance. By anchoring splendid feelings to fantastic physical or intellectual cues, athletes can cause self warranty and motivation every time they need it most. Reframing, however, includes converting the manner athletes understand tough situations. By viewing setbacks as possibilities for growth and mastering, athletes can keep a extraordinary mind-set and stay inspired even inside the face of adversity.

Furthermore, NLP strategies also can be applied to decorate conversation and relationships inside the sports sports activities surroundings. Effective conversation is essential for group sports activities, and NLP gives tools to beautify rapport-building, active listening, and information of non-verbal cues. By improving those abilties, athletes can foster better relationships with teammates, coaches, and different stakeholders, essential to a greater supportive and inspiring sports sports surroundings.

In stop, enhancing motivation and self belief in sports activities activities is critical for athletes to achieve top regular overall performance. NLP offers a variety of techniques and techniques that may be carried out sooner or later of severa niches, which include private development, agency and control, and sports activities sports general average overall performance enhancement. By incorporating NLP techniques which includes visualization, effective self-communicate, anchoring, reframing, and enhancing communique abilties, athletes can unfastened up their whole capacity, triumph over limitations, and excel of their selected undertaking. Whether you're an athlete, train, or sports sports activities enthusiast, the software program of NLP concepts in sports activities activities can empower you to acquire excellent consequences and obtain new heights on your sports activities adventure.

Visualizing Success and Achieving Peak Performance

Visualization is a powerful tool that would help people in all factors of their lives, from non-public improvement to agency and control, sports activities normal overall performance enhancement to overcoming phobias and fears, relationship and communique competencies to stress control and anxiety cut price, or maybe public speakme and presentation abilties, improving memory and getting to know talents, weight reduction and healthful manner of life, and fostering creativity and innovation.

In the region of Neuro Linguistic Programming (NLP), visualization performs a vital position in remodeling the mind and attaining peak not unusual ordinary performance. By harnessing the strength of the mind, human beings can create a intellectual picture of their preferred final outcomes and pressure themselves within the direction of achievement.

When visualizing success, one have to first choose out their dreams and goals. Whether it's far excelling in a particular sport, constructing better relationships, becoming a assured public speaker, or losing weight, the manner starts with a clean imaginative and prescient of what one desires to acquire. This clarity permits to direct the mind closer to the popular final results.

Once the motive is set up, the subsequent step is to create a bright intellectual photograph of the favored final results. This consists of using all of the senses to anticipate oneself already wearing out the goal. For instance, if the goal is to turn out to be a successful entrepreneur, one may additionally visualize themselves with a piece of accurate fortune pitching their business enterprise concept to potential buyers, feeling the pleasure in their achievement, and paying attention to the applause from the audience.

It is crucial to exercise this visualization regularly to enhance the popular final results in the thoughts. By over and over visualizing achievement, people can software program software their unconscious mind to believe in their abilities and growth their motivation to acquire this towards achieving their dreams.

In addition to visualization, strategies along side anchoring and reframing can further enhance the strength of visualization in NLP. Anchoring consists of associating a selected physical or highbrow kingdom with a favored outcome, on the same time as reframing allows humans reinterpret their reports in a greater remarkable and empowering way.

By incorporating visualization techniques into their day by day lives, individuals can faucet into the countless capability of their minds and acquire pinnacle basic performance in various regions. Whether it's miles improving their personal lives, excelling of their careers, or overcoming obstacles, the energy of visualization blended with NLP may be a transformative pressure.

Chapter 12: Nlp For Overcoming Phobias And Fears

Understanding the Root Causes of Phobias and Fears

Phobias and fears are common critiques that many human beings face of their ordinary lives. Whether it's miles a worry of heights, spiders, public speaking, or flying, the ones phobias may want to have a widespread impact on one's private and expert life. In order to overcome the ones fears and phobias, it is important to understand their root reasons and the manner they appear in our minds.

Neuro Linguistic Programming (NLP) gives precious insights into the underlying reasons of phobias and fears. NLP explores the relationship amongst our thoughts, language, and conduct, providing a framework for statistics how our minds technique and interpret fear-inducing stimuli.

One of the primary elements contributing to the development of phobias and fears is conditioning. Through past reviews or determined out behaviors, human beings may moreover partner positive gadgets or situations with fear or threat. For example, if someone had a annoying revel in with a dog as a infant, they will increase a phobia of dogs later in existence. NLP techniques can assist humans reframe these beyond memories and cast off the horrible associations, permitting them to technique the scary object or situation with a revel in of calm and control.

Another root purpose of phobias and fears is the manner we speak with ourselves. Our internal communicate and self-speak notably impact our perception of fear. Negative self-talk, collectively with constantly telling ourselves we aren't capable or properly worth, can intensify our fears and restriction our potential to triumph over them. NLP techniques can help individuals reprogram their internal talk, replacing horrific self-communicate with first rate affirmations and empowering beliefs, thereby decreasing the depth of their fears.

Additionally, phobias and fears are regularly deeply rooted inside the subconscious mind. Past traumas or unresolved feelings can create unconscious types of fear that hold to have an impact on our every day lives. NLP techniques, which encompass timeline treatment and anchoring, can help people get right of entry to and release the ones unconscious patterns, allowing them to interrupt loose from the grip of their phobias and fears.

Understanding the premise motives of phobias and fears is step one toward overcoming them. By utilising the requirements of Neuro Linguistic Programming, individuals can benefit insights into their conditioned responses, reframe terrible self-communicate, and release subconscious styles of fear. Whether for private development, commercial enterprise organization and manage, sports activities activities overall overall performance enhancement, or each distinct component of existence, NLP provides a powerful toolset for remodeling worry into empowerment and fulfillment.

Techniques for Overcoming Phobias and Fears

In this subchapter, we are able to discover diverse techniques from the arena of Neuro Linguistic Programming (NLP) that may assist human beings conquer their phobias and fears. Whether you're suffering with a fear of public talking, heights, spiders, or any other phobia, those techniques will let you take manipulate of your thoughts and emotions.

1. Anchoring:

Anchoring is a powerful NLP technique that lets in companion a incredible state with a particular motive. By growing an anchor, which include touching a particular part of your body, you could get admission to a fantastic emotional u.S.A. Every time you want it. This approach may be used to update worry with self guarantee, permitting you to face your phobias head-on.

2. Reframing:

Reframing is a manner that consists of changing the meaning or mindset of a scenario. By reframing your fears, you may adjust the way your thoughts perceives them. For instance, as opposed to viewing public speaking as a terrifying experience, you can reframe it as an interesting possibility to proportion your information and connect with others.

three. Visualization:

Visualization is a effective tool an awesome way to assist you to triumph over fears and phobias. By visualizing yourself effectively going thru your worry and feeling calm and assured, you may reprogram your mind to respond in a awesome way in real-life conditions. Regular exercise of visualization can assist desensitize you on your phobia and reduce anxiety.

four. Anchoring Resourceful States:

In addition to anchoring excessive terrific feelings, you could additionally anchor progressive states collectively with braveness, energy, and quietness. By using NLP strategies to create anchors for the ones states, you may get right of entry to them every time you need them maximum. This can be specially useful in conditions wherein your phobia or fear is triggered.

five. Timeline Therapy:

Timeline Therapy is an NLP technique that consists of revisiting beyond stories and reframing them. By liberating awful emotions associated with beyond demanding sports, you may loose your self from the grip of fear and phobias which could have advanced as a end end result. This method can help you allow move of the emotional bags that fuels your fears.

Overcoming phobias and fears is viable with the right mind-set and strategies. By incorporating the above NLP techniques into your personal improvement adventure, you could take control of your thoughts and conquer your fears. Whether you want to beautify your public speakme capabilities, triumph over a worry of flying, or any other phobia, NLP can provide you with the tool to convert your life. Embrace the strength of NLP and start your journey in the direction of a fearless and beautiful destiny.

Replacing Negative Associations with Positive Ones

In our journey within the course of private growth and development, it is crucial to recognize the electricity of our mind and establishments. Our minds have the great ability to shape our fact, and thru the exercising of Neuro Linguistic Programming (NLP), we're able to harness this strength to convert our lives.

Negative establishments can save you our improvement and hold us trapped in styles of self-sabotage. These institutions are long-established thru past studies, traumas, or perhaps societal conditioning. However, it's far interior our manipulate to replace those awful institutions with excellent ones.

One of the vital techniques of NLP is reframing, which includes changing the meaning and perspective of an enjoy. By reframing terrible critiques, we're capable of shift our reputation towards the exquisite elements and extract precious education from them. This technique permits us to break free from the restrictions of horrible establishments and rewire our minds for fulfillment.

In the realm of personal improvement, this method may be applied to numerous areas of our lives. Whether it's overcoming phobias and fears, enhancing relationships and verbal exchange abilities, handling strain and anxiety, or enhancing creativity and innovation, reframing poor establishments is a powerful tool.

In the business and control sphere, NLP can help people update limiting beliefs with empowering ones. By reframing past screw ups as treasured studying opinions, leaders can domesticate resilience and encourage their agencies to gain greatness. Similarly, in sports sports overall overall performance enhancement, athletes can reframe setbacks as opportunities for boom, allowing them to push beyond their limits and gather new heights.

Moreover, NLP can also be beneficial in improving reminiscence and analyzing competencies. By replacing terrible institutions with effective ones, we're able to beautify our functionality to keep statistics and boost up our mastering method. Additionally, within the pursuit of a wholesome way of life or weight loss, reframing can help us increase a awesome relationship with food and exercising, main to sustainable behavior and lasting alternate.

For the ones struggling with public speakme and presentation capabilities, NLP strategies may be profitable. By reframing nervousness as exhilaration and fear as anticipation, individuals can harness their strength and supply impactful speeches with self belief.

By records the strength of our institutions and the usage of NLP strategies including reframing, we will remodel our lives in exceptional strategies. Whether it's miles in personal development, commercial enterprise and control, sports activities basic overall performance enhancement, overcoming fears, or enhancing severa elements of our lives, NLP offers sensible tools to replace horrible establishments with remarkable ones. Embracing this exercising enables us to recognize our minds and create the life we actually preference.

Building Resilience and Confidence in Facing Fears

Fear is a commonplace emotion that everyone opinions ultimately of their lives. Whether it is the concern of failure, rejection, or the unknown, it can keep us lower back from carrying out our full functionality. However, via information and enforcing the ideas of Neuro Linguistic Programming (NLP), we can discover ways to assemble resilience and self guarantee in going thru our fears.

NLP offers a effective toolkit for private improvement, corporation management, sports activities performance enhancement, overcoming phobias and fears, relationship and communication talents, strain control and tension discount, public talking and presentation capabilities, improving reminiscence and analyzing talents, weight loss and healthy way of lifestyles, further to creativity and innovation enhancement. By making use of NLP strategies, we're capable of rework our mind-set and triumph over the restrictions that worry imposes on us.

Chapter 13: Nlp For Relationship And Communication Skills

Improving Interpersonal Communication with NLP

Effective interpersonal communique is critical for achievement in different factors of lifestyles, whether or not it's far in non-public relationships, organization interactions, public speaking, or maybe sports activities sports everyday ordinary performance. Neuro Linguistic Programming (NLP) offers powerful equipment and techniques to beautify communication capabilities and foster good sized connections with others.

In this subchapter, we are capable of discover how NLP may be applied to decorate interpersonal conversation in numerous contexts, catering to a numerous target market with pursuits starting from personal improvement to weight reduction and creativity enhancement. Regardless of your area of interest, NLP can provide treasured insights and strategies to enhance your communique talents.

One essential factor of NLP is understanding the electricity of language. By becoming aware of the phrases we use and the impact they've got on ourselves and others, we can start to redesign our communique styles. NLP teaches us to choose out our phrases cautiously, using excessive satisfactory and empowering language to create rapport, assemble do not forget, and encourage change.

Another key principle of NLP is knowing and using non-verbal communication. Our frame language, facial expressions, and tone of voice can supply more than phrases on my own. By reading to look at and reply to non-verbal cues, we're able to better recognize others and adjust our very very own conduct to create a extra harmonious and effective verbal exchange system.

NLP additionally emphasizes active listening abilities, which can be essential for effective interpersonal verbal exchange. By genuinely listening to and expertise others, we will reply empathetically and make certain that our message is acquired because it must be. NLP strategies which consist of mirroring and matching may be used to set up rapport and create a revel in of reference to others.

Furthermore, NLP offers powerful strategies for overcoming phobias and fears, reducing strain and anxiety, enhancing memory and getting to know talents, and even selling a healthful lifestyle. By making use of NLP strategies in those regions, we will decorate our common nicely-being and, consequently, our functionality to talk correctly with others.

Whether you are seeking to enhance your personal relationships, excel in industrial corporation and control, decorate your sports activities activities ordinary ordinary performance, or become a more confident public speaker, NLP has the gear and strategies that will help you acquire your dreams. By analyzing the artwork of interpersonal communication via NLP, you could revel in more success and success in all regions of your life.

In the subsequent chapters, we're capable of delve deeper into unique applications of NLP in every vicinity of interest, providing realistic sporting activities and real-existence examples to guide you for your adventure to studying your thoughts and improving your interpersonal communique competencies.

Active Listening and Empathy Building Techniques

In the place of Neuro Linguistic Programming (NLP), the energy of effective communique cannot be overstated. Whether you're looking for private boom, professional fulfillment, or stronger standard normal performance in severa areas of lifestyles, reading energetic listening and empathy building strategies is essential.

Active listening is the art work of clearly attractive with others, now not definitely listening to their words however truely information their mind, feelings, and perspectives. By actively listening, we will set up deeper connections, build believe, and foster significant relationships. This expertise is worthwhile in all factors of lifestyles, be it private relationships, employer interactions, or perhaps sports sports overall performance enhancement.

Empathy, however, is the functionality to step into someone else's footwear and certainly apprehend their studies and emotions. Empathy lets in us to connect to others on a profound degree, imparting guide and steerage which can result in transformative alternate. Whether you are helping a person conquer a fear or constructing a more potent relationship, empathy is a powerful device.

To cultivate energetic listening competencies, start by giving your entire hobby to the speaker. Avoid distractions and reputation on their phrases, tone, and frame language. Show actual hobby with the aid of manner of preserving eye touch, nodding, and the use of verbal cues to inspire them to percentage more. Practice reflective listening via paraphrasing what they have got said to make certain knowledge and to allow them to understand you're truely engaged.

Empathy building strategies involve actively looking to apprehend any other character's mind-set. Put yourself of their shoes and try to don't forget how they is probably feeling. Ask open-ended inquiries to inspire them to unique themselves and validate their emotions. Avoid judging or disregarding their opinions and as an alternative offer useful resource and data.

By analyzing lively listening and empathy building techniques, you may beautify your private and expert relationships, decorate your capacity to communicate successfully, and attain achievement in diverse areas of existence. Whether you are looking to conquer phobias and fears, reduce strain and tension, or beautify your public talking and presentation talents, those talents is probably treasured.

In quit, energetic listening and empathy constructing are critical capabilities inside the worldwide of NLP. These techniques permit us to hook up with others on a deeper diploma, fostering personal boom, improving professional fulfillment, and enhancing different factors of life. Whether you are attempting to find non-public development, commercial enterprise control, sports activities common performance enhancement, or some different area of development, integrating those strategies into your communique toolkit will actually yield transformative consequences.

Resolving Conflict and Building Healthy Relationships

In our adventure toward personal improvement and growth, it's miles inevitable that we come upon conflicts and challenges in our relationships. Whether it's far with our loved ones, colleagues, or even inner ourselves, battle can regularly prevent our development and ward off the fulfillment of our desires. However, with the power of Neuro Linguistic Programming (NLP), we're capable of examine powerful techniques to solve warfare and construct wholesome relationships.

NLP gives a totally precise set of equipment and strategies that allow us to apprehend the underlying dynamics of struggle and communique. By mastering NLP, we're capable of select out and alter our personal styles of wondering, feeling, and behaving that make contributions to battle. Through this gadget, we are able to gain a deeper information of ourselves and others, fostering empathy and compassion in our relationships.

One of the important thing concepts of NLP is the recognition that everybody has their private specific version of the sector. By acknowledging and respecting these differences, we are capable of set up a robust foundation for powerful verbal exchange and struggle desire. NLP teaches us to listen actively, in search of to recognize the views and wishes of others. Through this empathetic approach, we're able to bridge the gaps of false impression and find out common floor for selection.

Furthermore, NLP equips us with effective techniques for handling our emotions and responses in some unspecified time in the future of conflicts. By using device collectively with anchoring and reframing, we're able to shift our thoughts-set and emotional usa, permitting us to stay calm and composed inside the face of struggle. This capacity to adjust our feelings and preserve a rational attitude lets in us to approach conflicts with readability and objectivity.

In addition to resolving warfare, NLP additionally emphasizes the significance of constructing wholesome relationships. Through NLP, we will growth effective conversation skills that foster receive as real with, apprehend, and understanding. By mastering rapport building strategies, we will installation sturdy connections with others, developing a sturdy foundation for collaboration and cooperation.

Ultimately, NLP offers a complete framework for resolving war and constructing healthy relationships. By using the requirements and strategies of NLP, we are able to transform conflicts into opportunities for growth and information. Whether in personal relationships, commercial enterprise enterprise settings, or sports activities sports sports standard common performance, NLP equips us with the gadget to navigate conflicts with grace and create harmonious relationships.

No depend your region of interest, whether or not or not or not you're looking for to improve your communication abilities, conquer fears and phobias, control strain and anxiety, or decorate your control abilities, NLP is a transformative tool that would revolutionize your relationships and pave the manner for private and professional fulfillment. Join us on this journey of analyzing your thoughts thru NLP and find out the strength to treatment conflicts and assemble healthy relationships.

Enhancing Non-Verbal Communication Skills

In the region of Neuro Linguistic Programming (NLP), mastering non-verbal communique skills is of excessive significance. Non-verbal verbal exchange encompasses the subtle but effective signs we deliver and acquire through body language, facial expressions, gestures, and tone of voice. These non-verbal cues often deliver our proper mind and feelings, even more so than our terms.

Chapter 14: Nlp For Stress Management And Anxiety Reduction

Understanding the Effects of Stress and Anxiety

Stress and anxiety are commonplace factors that have an impact on human beings from all walks of existence. Whether you are an athlete striving for top common overall performance, a employer professional searching out achievement, or someone searching for to enhance their personal relationships, know-how the results of stress and tension is crucial in learning your thoughts and wearing out your dreams.

In the world of Neuro Linguistic Programming (NLP), strain and anxiety are visible as emotional responses that can keep away from private increase and success. When we revel in stress, our bodies launch hormones that prepare us for a fight-or-flight response. While this reaction can be beneficial in excessive satisfactory situations, prolonged pressure can result in physical and highbrow fitness problems.

Anxiety, as an alternative, is a greater continual scenario characterized thru excessive worrying, restlessness, and a enjoy of coming close to close to doom. It ought to have a profound impact on our thoughts, feelings, and behaviors, making it tough to characteristic optimally in diverse areas of existence.

NLP gives some of techniques and techniques to assist people control and conquer stress and tension. By data the underlying kinds of the ones emotions, we will reprogram our minds to reply differently and create more empowering states of being.

For example, NLP strategies like anchoring and reframing can be used to interrupt horrible idea patterns and update them with superb ones. By anchoring ourselves to a innovative u . S ., we are able to shift our popularity some distance from pressure and anxiety and rather faucet right into a country of calmness and self warranty.

Additionally, NLP offers device for dealing with strain and anxiety in unique contexts. If you struggle with public speaking or indicates, NLP strategies can help you reframe your ideals and adopt empowering strategies to triumph over your worry and deliver impactful speeches. Similarly, if you are an athlete looking to beautify your overall performance, NLP permit you to control pre-competition nerves and develop a winning mind-set.

Ultimately, information the effects of strain and anxiety is important for personal improvement, industrial corporation fulfillment, sports overall performance enhancement, and numerous other areas of life. By using the thoughts and strategies of NLP, human beings can benefit control over their feelings, lessen strain and tension, and free up their complete capacity. Whether you attempting to find strain control, advanced verbal exchange competencies, weight loss, or creativity enhancement, NLP offers a whole toolkit to help you master your thoughts and achieve your goals.

Techniques for Stress Relief and Relaxation

Stress has end up an inevitable part of our speedy-paced lives, affecting our highbrow, emotional, and bodily well-being. It is crucial for people from all walks of life to research effective strategies for pressure remedy and rest. Whether you are attempting to beautify your personal improvement, enhance your company and control skills, excel in sports frequent performance, triumph over phobias and fears, enhance your relationship and conversation competencies, manipulate stress and tension, supply assured public speeches, beautify your memory and mastering capabilities, attain weight loss and a healthful manner of existence, or beautify your creativity and innovation, Neuro Linguistic Programming (NLP) offers a number of powerful strategies that will help you achieve those dreams.

One such method is known as "Anchoring." Anchoring is a system that allows you to associate a specific intellectual or emotional united states of america with a physical stimulus. By growing an anchor, which include a hint or a selected gesture, you may trigger immoderate excellent states of relaxation and calmness whenever you need them. This method may be especially useful for handling pressure and tension in numerous conditions, whether or not or not it's miles inside the administrative center, in the course of public speaking engagements, or in personal relationships.

www.ingramcontent.com/pod-product-compliance
Lightning Source LLC
Chambersburg PA
CBHW071444080526
44587CB00014B/1991